STONE WORK

DESIGNING WITH STONE BY MALCOLM HOLZMAN

First published in Australia in 2001 by
The Images Publishing Group Pty Ltd ACN 059 734 431
6 Bastow Place, Mulgrave, Victoria, 3170, Australia
Telephone (61 3) 9561 5544 Facsimile (61 3) 9561 4860
Email: books@images.com.au Website: www.imagespublishinggroup.com

The National Library of Australia Cataloguing-in-Publication Data
Holtzman, Macolm.

Designing for stone.

ISBN 1 86470 083 1.

1. Building stones. 2. Stone. 3. Building materials.
4. Architectural design. I. Title.

691.2

Text by Malcolm Holzman
Book Design by Henry Holtzman
Cover photography by Denny Tillman
Production artwork by The Graphic Image Studio Pty Ltd, Australia
Printed in China by Everbest Printing

STONE WORK

DISCARDED

DESIGNING WITH STONE BY MALCOLM HOLZMAN

TEXT BY MALCOLM HOLZMAN

BOOK DESIGN BY HENRY HOLTZMAN

Slate fence, Caithness, Scotland

We are all that we have done. It will all come back.
– Carlos Fuentes

Architects must look within themselves to determine what they want to do—what is their passion.
– Henry Hobson Richardson

Dakota granite remnant wall, University of Nebraska at Omaha Fine Arts Building

Stones are dead things sleeping in the quarries but the apses of St. Peter's are a drama.
— Le Corbusier

Talking about music is like dancing about architecture.
— Thelonious Monk

Dry-stone wall, Yorkshire, England

INTRODUCTION

Favorable circumstances and personal inclination have enabled me to explore the use of stone as a building material. As a college student with a toothed chisel and hammer, I found stone harder to shape than wood and much less forgiving than clay. Even so, its finished volumetric surfaces—which conveyed visual impressions—also imparted irresistible tactile sensations. I learned that it was possible to reveal stone's mass and weight with elegance as Michelangelo did in his six Slaves, a series of sculptures in which the figures emerge from massive marble blocks. Their capacity to seem both rough-hewn and unfinished, as well

as highly refined and complete, made a lasting impression. Achieving analogous results in architecture was an early aspiration; it remains in the forefront of my thinking to this day. Stone's richness of texture, color and finish cannot be found in other materials.

Until the beginning of the twentieth century, an architect's training had a defined course. Individuals interested in taking it up as a profession became apprentices. Working with a skilled master, interns honed their craft until thoroughly learning how to bring a building to life by transcending standard applications. The demise of this

system ended the kind of master-apprentice relationship established centuries ago when Nicholas Hawksmoor worked in Sir Christopher Wren's studio, or when Stanford White was employed by Henry Hobson Richardson.

Today, aspiring architects are taught at academic institutions where scholarship is based on mastering factual information and exposure to actual building experiences is limited. In many cases the primary goal of architectural education is the activity itself and preparing individuals for making buildings can be secondary. In addition to formal academic programs a novice can navigate through the

architectural wilderness by studying the work of the masters and searching for historic examples that are still capable of physically conveying the designers' intent. They can also investigate the materials of construction to become proficient at determining their virtues or deficiencies. And they can consider evolving technology that is making materials and construction even more versatile. Doing all these, often independently, is essential to gaining the knowledge to entertain a career in architecture.

Stone is not a vanishing natural resource. Actually, the opposite is true. Its advance as a building product is

constrained only by the user. Making architecture with this material often requires putting aside accepted strictures and finding a means to work with, and understand, its physical qualities. In the past, stone has proven to be an infinitely adaptable substance. Currently, taking the time and effort to reflect on effectively using it in a building may seem daunting. For me it has proven to be a most rewarding exercise. The longer I look at it, examine it, and deliberate on its potential for a project, the better I become at divining its possibilities. Finding new variants for materials is a recurrent theme in my work.

Stone can be more than a symbol of historic buildings that conjures the handing down of embalmed design styles, the propagation of archaic customs, or our current national enthusiasm for nostalgia. In a time when there is as much interest in the past as the present, flashback architecture can be too easy a bromide. Familiarity with techniques of quarrying, cutting and erecting stone is essential if the architect is to avoid adopting styles and practices that have exceeded their usefulness. Working on the principle that the continued evolution of stone buildings will lead to architecture's possessing a full and consistent meaning for

our times, I strive to take advantage of current methods for fabrication and installation—along with reinvigorated existing ones.

This publication is arranged thematically rather than chronologically or geologically. Instructions for building with stone are not presented; they should come out of the fundamental ideas of a design. Instead, I have included vignettes about observing antiquities as well as commonplace structures and about manufacturing stone and making buildings. These can be seen as episodic incidents—which recall only the general aspects of my projects—

focusing on the role stone can play in making exceptional architecture. My intention is to demonstrate not only that the application of stone can still result in architecture unlike that created from other materials, but also that it can be of more interest today than it has been in the recent past. To raise public awareness about the material and to influence architects to redirect their attention to stone is my objective. They will discover, as I have, that it is sensuous to the touch, striking to the eye, and pleasing to the soul.

Malcolm Holzman, July 4, 2001.

12-sided Stone, Cuzco, Peru

TOUCHSTONE

Stone monolith, Ring of Brodgar, Orkney, Scotland

TOUCHSTONE

It is hard to imagine world architecture without Neolithic megaliths, Egyptian pyramids, Greek temples, Roman baths, Gothic cathedrals, and Renaissance palazzos that portray its evolution. The narrative record of architecture and stone began thousands of years ago with huge, uncarved boulders erected on ceremonial sites. Structures with massive walls and roofs followed. Their thick cyclopean character was relieved—over time—by columns, arches and vaults. Large and frequent openings appeared in walls as buildings became multi-storied. Made of stone from the geographical area where they were conceived and erected, these structures convey the distinct characteristics and spirit of each locale.

The succession of construction techniques applied to stone buildings is as diverse as the history of architecture itself. The mason's role progressed with each new way of using the material, from the erection of dry-set rubble walls to the application of mortar between cut blocks. Whether the hammer and chisel produced rough blocks or tooled recessed joints, building units were undeniably handmade and carefully set in place. The imprint of the stone-cutter and mason provided human scale to the structures. Building with stone evolved through an apprenticeship system that allowed practitioners to improve their skills and to carry them forward from one generation to the next.

Because of its availability, durability, and strength, stone was long the first choice for exterior building surfaces. But from early in the nineteenth century to the middle of the twentieth century, manufactured products began to erode its pre-eminence. Competition arose from the novel application of terracotta, brick, concrete block, glass, metal, and plastics, which could be readily manufactured as part of a repetitive industrial process, transported long distances, and simply installed. As the shift from stone to other materials took place, older building types gave way to new ones with less three-dimensional relief.

A procession of American architectural styles—classical revival, prairie style, art moderne, and art deco—led to a modernism that did away with the illusion of depth. Abstract, gridded, geometric volumes and even, smooth, uniform façades were preferable to those with texture, pattern, ornament, shade and shadow. A flat surface was considered superior to a three-dimensional one, and a flat surface with minimal detail was deemed even better.

Though stone suppliers and fabricators pushed production limits in an attempt to accommodate the popular streamlined aesthetic, they could neither contend with the lower cost of other materials nor with modernism's

Standing Stones of Callanish, Isle of Lewis, Scotland

partiality to flatness. They needed a completely new point of departure to compete with other products. Two innovations, one in stone processing and the other in enhanced adhesives, gave manufacturers a suitable means to cope with their rivals. Machinery capable of cutting stone almost membrane-thin allowed it to become a component of panelized wall systems. This type of

application could dispense with masons for installation, and materials could be assembled far from construction sites.

While panels can be anchored to buildings of any height, they bear little resemblance to stone's origin as a building material, giving no particular insight into its inherent properties. In this minimal form, stone looks anonymous and appears drained of the qualities that make it

Karnak, Egypt

a remarkable product. Many panelized buildings also lapsed into hackneyed renditions of imagery gleaned from previous eras. It took three decades—from 1960 to 1990—to transform the production of stone from cubic blocks and mortar to panels, adhesives, and no mortar. This is now the most subscribed-to method for using the material because architects seek substitutes for resources considered costly

and are inclined to depend on the most widely accepted applications.

For the current modernism to evolve, the use of stone should move beyond the expediency of panelization. It should embrace new technology and economics but it should also incorporate ways to espouse the lyricism, beauty and human qualities that stone so eloquently expresses.

Cathedral Notre Dame de Paris

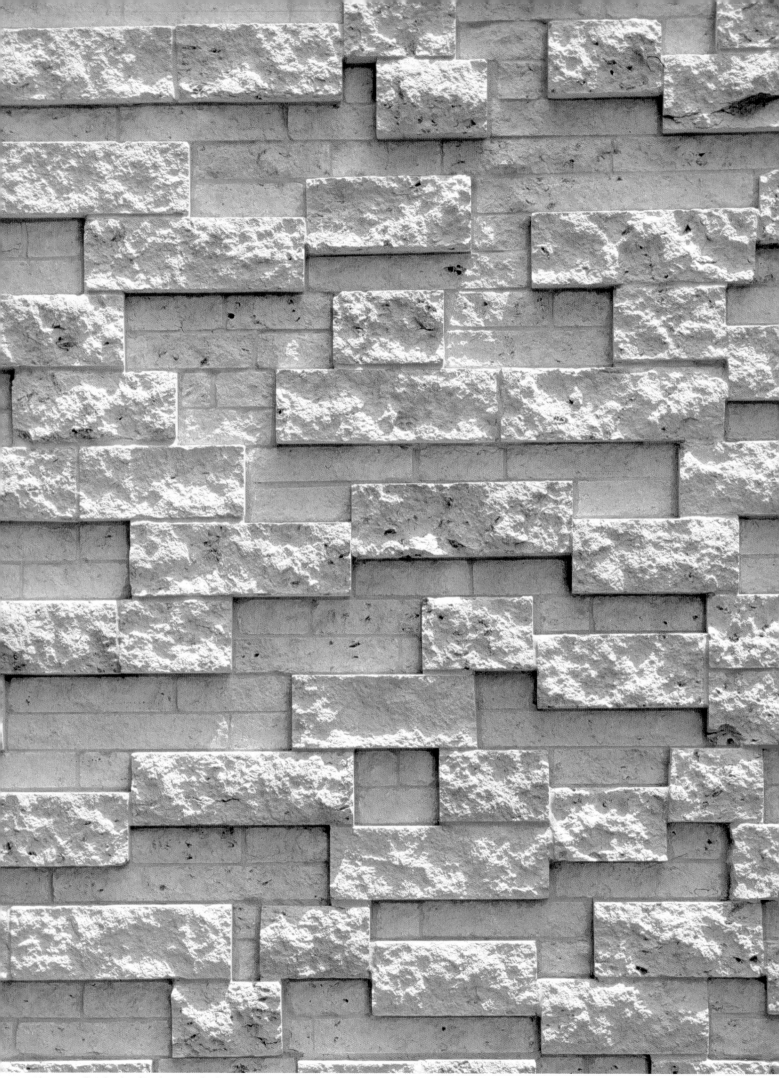

Limestone wall, University of North Texas Performing Arts Center

Lobby, University of North Texas Performing Arts Center

Entry walkway, University of North Texas Performing Arts Center

Lobby, University of North Texas Performing Arts Center

View from Interstate 35, University of North Texas Performing Arts Center

Boulders at the gas station, Madonna Inn, Alex Madonna

GRINDSTONE

GRINDSTONE

In its most compelling form, stone imparts color, texture and diversity. And at its most finished, it can be smooth, reflective, undulating and even lush. These distinctive qualities, along with many others, should be exploited, not minimized. Today, designers can choose from a wider range of sources and applications for stone than in any other era.

A long-standing interest of mine has been the expression of the underlying characteristics of the material: mass, weight, and gravity. Numerous architects have explored these properties, and a limited number during the last century communicated these attributes in original ways. These designers may be better known for who they are than what they did. Regardless of style, they developed building projects that transmitted their personal interests and concurrently advanced the use of the material, sometimes with unexpected results.

In Cleveland, Ohio, the Society National Bank (now the Key Bank) designed by John Wellborn Root in 1894, reflects the era's enthusiasm, energy and industrial prowess, as well as the architect's sophisticated understanding of masonry construction. Only slightly taller than it is wide, this nearly cubic structure still serves as a bank, more than one hundred years after its opening. It has survived a 1960s' alteration to its nine-story central light well, a 1990s' restoration program, and an adjacent hi-rise expansion. Today, the red sandstone exterior walls, although liberally punctuated by openings, still allude to gravity's compressive force in its ingenuous details. The uniform ten-story building façades meet a series of short, intentionally stocky columns just before they touch down on the north side of Public Square, the city's most ceremonial outdoor space. The columns, disproportionately wide for their diminutive height, support the façades on rough-hewn, Romanesque-inspired undecorated capitals. One detail distinguishes this building from all others constructed in its time. At the classical torus-shaped column bases, occupying a band less than two inches high, the architect has superimposed four griffes. These languid, carved leaves - unlike the solidified works of nature sometimes found in Gothic structures - more closely resemble liquefied mortar forced out between the column and its base by the weight of the robust building above. This notable structure contrasts rough-hewn stone blocks with refined features, exemplifying Root's ability to employ the style of the period while fancifully expressing the force of gravity.

Halfway up the California coast from Los Angeles to San Francisco there is a great place to spend the night — the

Column base griffes, Society National Bank, John Wellborn Root

Madonna Inn. Constructed incrementally, starting in 1958, by its owner, Alex Madonna, it is, like many other Californian motels, "themed," thus making it a popular destination. Similarities with other tourist spots along the way end here, though, because of the owner's quixotic, adroit and particular use of stone. Giant boulders are carefully placed, appearing next to gas pumps, under wood

stairs and walkways, and - most startlingly - in guestrooms. Visitors can select, through a series of picture postcards or on the Internet, the type of rock "feature" with which they want to spend the night. Kitschy but endearing, this rest spot takes the material we know well and uses it in an idiosyncratic way that is emblematic of California culture. Reversing conventional practice, the stone supports

Gas station, Madonna Inn, Alex Madonna

1990 pavillion additions to 1912 building, Middlebury College Student Activities Center

Clapboard and granite addition, Middlebury College Student Activities Center

Curb stone granite façade details, Middlebury College Student Activities Center

nothing, but decorates everything, creating a series of singular environments. When my family and I first encountered these accessories, we broke into smiles of surprise and delight.

In 1968, during the height of the American Modernist movement, the firm Kevin Roche John Dinkeloo and Associates was commissioned by Wesleyan University to design a building whose program included three auditoriums. There was a one-hundred-fifty-year tradition of constructing modestly scaled structures in this open, green, six-acre collegiate setting. Eschewing the design of one large blocky building, the architects made a series of limestone structures connected by paths and dispersed them across the campus. To make these units appear smaller than they are, a number of the larger volumetric spaces were placed partially below grade.

In this way, these separate, seemingly small stone structures relate to the existing series of buildings. The new ones do not defer to the old but take their place alongside them in the additive practice of this institution. Coincidentally, at the time of construction, sawn cubic limestone blocks - three-feet-eight inches by two-feet-six inches by fourteen inches - proved economical as a structural bearing wall for these buildings. The firm's ability to use stone when exposed concrete was the order of the day is as remarkable as the placement of these objects. In addition to its use as a structural material, the limestone's coursing, block patterns and sawn finish provide the only decoration. These well-placed minimalist structures correspond to their neighbors, but in an unflinching way, even while they become part of an older tradition.

The four walls enclosing the Cistercian Abbey Church in Irving, Texas are composed of four hundred twenty-seven stone quarry blocks and mortar. Six by three by two feet and weighing about two and a half tons each, these blocks were erected as structural walls (similar to those previously described at Wesleyan). The roof that bears on these walls is as straightforward as the building beneath it – constructed with wooden beams, decking, and steel tie rods. Although visually defined by merely three elements - stone, wood, and light - the building is not like any other 250-seat chapel that a congregant might attend for worship.

This sanctuary has more in common with European cathedrals than its 1980s Texas contemporaries. Gary Cunningham, the architect, has designed its space with a single withe of materials and natural light, giving it a medieval augustness that belies its small size.

Sawn limestone blocks, Wesleyan University Arts Building, Kevin Roche John Dinkeloo and Associates

Functional and technical requirements were considered in these projects and resolved with a combination of ingenuity and expertise. Each of the designers employed large stone blocks, not as an end in itself or to achieve pragmatic requirements. They selected stone to impart special qualities in each undertaking — gravity, humor, scale and atmosphere — confirming that architects exploit stone to endow buildings with human interest and to supply each structure with its essential character.

Quarry block walls, Cistercian Abbey Church, Gary Cunningham

West Wing, Virginia Museum of Fine Arts

View from University Drive, University of the South McClurg Hall

Dakota granite remant blocks, University of Nebraska at Omaha Fine Arts Building

STEPPING STONE

STEPPING STONE

Mark Twain's Innocents Abroad is a high-spirited, pretension-deflating chronicle of a European grand tour. Though it was published in 1869, this entertaining account of a journey to celebrated destinations still demonstrates that while travel can broaden our thinking and expose us to new cultures, understanding what we observe is a haphazard process. In fact, the traveler may well encounter one thing while looking for another.

Frequently, the remains at a historic building site are fragmentary. Fitting bits and pieces of divergent information into a coherent framework may be demanding, but the moments of spontaneous perception are well worth the effort. Antiquities and anomalies discovered first-hand hold a special place in my affection. Insights about construction and stone that initially appeared unrelated have influenced my professional outlook. Knowledge gained at nearby and far-flung destinations emerge in unusual ways in my work.

In 1980, I visited the popular tourist site in Aswan, Egypt, where 3500 years ago, the Egyptians quarried and fabricated obelisks. One of these—an unfinished red granite block weighing more than two million pounds—had been left in its original quarry location, where trenches around it showed signs of the removal operation. It had been cut from the surrounding stone on five out of six sides, and only the bottom remained anchored to its bed. However, prior to the final step in the quarrying process, numerous fissures developed in this long narrow block, preventing the obelisk from being snapped free in its entirety. Seeing this abandoned object was a galvanic experience because it conveyed that the procedure for removing stone from quarries has not changed significantly in 35 centuries. It also prompted me to journey to other quarry and fabrication locations all over the world.

I came to believe that a stone's idiosyncrasies could best be perceived by studying the material at the source, where the circumstances surrounding its extraction are easily grasped. Personal knowledge of the methods employed at quarries and fabrication shops is invaluable to the architect in determining the way stone can ultimately be used in a building project. Although methods for removing the material from the ground may be comparable from one quarry to the next, each stone's individuality is most discernible at the place where it originates.

One revelation from such a visit came during a search for materials to clad the new Luanne and Del Webber Fine Arts Building at the University of Nebraska, in Omaha, whose

---

Recumbent obelisk, Aswan, Egypt

construction budget was just over $115 per square foot in 1992. With such a modest budget, not many materials initially seemed affordable. For more than a century, a series of quarries along an extended stone deposit in central South Dakota have been a well-known source of material in the upper Midwest. I first read about granite from this area in an advertisement. A subsequent telephone call provided

enough information to prompt a visit to the quarry and fabrication operations in Milbank.

My initial tour of Dakota Granite's operations included a stop at the quarry pit, an inspection of the fabrication shop where new cutting and polishing equipment had just been installed, and a look at stored material. One of the products manufactured is a dark red, almost mahogany-colored,

Dakota granite quarry

Dakota granite, Minnesota limestone and brick building components, University of Nebraska at Omaha Fine Arts Building cemetery headstone. The production process requires the finishing of entire slabs of the material to determine its usability as a monument and some are rejected following final inspection. I was particularly interested in these eight-inch thick pieces polished on both sides. These rejects could be sent through a splitter to make eight- by four-inch building blocks in random lengths. This material not only

looked good, but the price was hard to ignore. At $80 a ton, its cost was almost comparable to brick. At my request, a few pieces from the split granite rejects were piled up to simulate a wall condition. Provided that special attention was given at the time of installation to the random lengths of the material, this was a usable product for the exterior walls of the building's art gallery and theater.

Minnesota limestone quoins and concrete north entrance, University of Nebraska at Omaha Fine Arts Building

Minnesota limestone quoins and concrete, University of Nebraska at Omaha Fine Arts Building

Minnesota limestone tower and clinker brick studio wing, University of Nebraska at Omaha Fine Arts Building

During a series of visits to the highlands of Scotland,
I became aware that some of the internal functions of
baronial buildings are visible on the outside, just as external
forms may appear in the interior. The easiest to discern from
the outside are the turnpike stairs. Their cylindrical form,
usually topped with a conical roof, is one of the identifying
elements that make these buildings distinctive. On the

interior, stair-tower enclosures are also hard to miss as
their curved walls nip off the corner of a rectangular room.
The discovery of an exterior building form within a structure
serves as a landmark for the visitor. In these residences, one
always knows where the stairs are and can make a quick exit
if necessary.

The public projects I design frequently employ a similar
stratagem to orient large groups of visitors. Many of my

Craigievar Castle, Scotland

Granite, clay tile and brick frame at west entry, Texas Christian University Center for Performing Arts

Granite and clay tile theater enclosure, Texas Christian University Center for Performing Arts

Limestone, clay tile and travertine east façade, Texas Christian University Center for Performing Arts

recent buildings rely on open plans to provide economy in construction and multiple uses for a given area. The circulation spaces often derive their shape from the three-dimensional volumes that surround them, like tower stairs. For example, Texas red granite and structural clay tile clad the exterior walls of the Hays Studio Theatre at Texas Christian University's Walsh Center, in Fort Worth. From the outside, these warm-colored materials mark the north entry to the building and can be seen at the end of a long campus vista that terminates a residential quadrangle. Portions of these walls are visible inside, in the building's multilevel lobby, and, being instantly identifiable, direct patrons to the theater.

In the late 1800s, H. H. Richardson developed a style of masonry construction so distinct that it took his name and is now known as Richardson Romanesque. He used massive, rough-cut stone blocks with limited openings to sheath buildings. One illustration is the large, arched opening in the otherwise blank penitentiary façade of the Allegheny County Courthouse in Pittsburgh, Pennsylvania. In the composition of his libraries and churches, a different American vision was realized. In these structures, Richardson contrasted a variety of finishes and materials. At the tower of Grace Church in Medford, Massachusetts,

all the way to the top of the steeple, smooth bands of stone alternate with rubble ones, visually extending its height and dimensions. This juxtaposition accentuates both finishes, enlivens a large expanse and shifts the scale of the steeple from the individual stone units to the larger bands.

I have adopted a practice comparable to Richardson's use of harmonious and dissonant finishes and materials in a single building. Connecting or contrasting warm to cool, regular to random, or rough to smooth can deliver a distinct personality to a structure, lending identity to exterior building elements and interior spaces. Two glazed stair enclosures and a central portal are the only three-dimensional accents to the 300-foot long West Wing façade of the Virginia Museum of Fine Arts in Richmond. To protect the artwork within, minimal window openings and strict control of natural light were requirements for this sizable addition. A voluptuous, bullnose limestone section tops three courses of 30-inch high, rusticated blocks to form a continuous base for this façade. Rising from this point to the top of the parapet are alternating courses of shot sawn and tooled pieces of limestone. Twelve feet shy of the top, two polished granite courses surround one rusticated limestone band corresponding to the differing cornice

Granite arch, Allegheny County Courthouse, H.H. Richardson

Rubble and cut stone, Grace Church, H.H. Richardson

Limestone and glass, Virginia Museum of Fine Arts, West Wing

Exit terrace, Albert Paley gate, Westside Highway lamp post and Claes Oldenburg Clothespin, Virginia Museum of Fine Arts, West Wing

Bullnose and rusticated limestone, Virginia Museum of Fine Arts, West Wing

Mock-up of marble wall in fabricator's yard, Virginia Museum of Fine Arts, West Wing

Marble wall and axial entry, Virginia Museum of Fine Arts, West Wing

Marble floor, stair and wall with Texas shellstone columns, Virginia Museum of Fine Arts, West Wing

Sawn and tooled limestone blocks and polished granite surrounding rusticated band, Virginia Museum of Fine Arts, West Wing

heights on the adjoining neo-Georgian museum structures. The variation in adjoining surfaces does not need to be great to enliven a building's façades. In this case, the limestone is uniform in color, while the contrasting textures, finishes and shapes provide for the changes in value as sunlight cascades across its lively surfaces.

During a recent trip to Peru's Urabamba River Valley, I visited Inca constructions that frequently incorporated the stone of the mountainsides into the structures. They shaped their buildings to the contour of the hillsides, creating singular objects seamed together from fabricated stone and natural outcroppings. This approach to locating buildings in the landscape differs from the standard American method for

Mountainside outcrop cut to receive stone blocks, Monolito, de Q'enqo, Peru

Stone terraces along Urubamba River, Peru

preparing sites for construction. Most often, all vegetation is removed, and then significant ground contours are bulldozed away. The idealized site for development is flat or gently sloping with no encumbrances.

The relationship of a building to the land on which it sits is a strong consideration in my work. Whenever possible, I accept the physical conditions of the site as a determinant for design and construction, and I bring the structure to the ground contour or gently shape the ground to accept the building. At Creighton University's Lied Education Center for the Arts in Omaha, Nebraska for example, the internal functions of the building were arranged to take advantage of the 30-foot slope at this particular campus location. External access is linked to building activities on three sides of the structure at three different levels. Two portals are located along a major campus pedestrian thoroughfare at the lower level, providing easy passage to teaching spaces; a formal drive-up entry allows community visitors direct access to major performance and gallery spaces at mid level; and a separate secure entry for ceramic and sculpture materials is located at the highest level in an outdoor kiln yard and work area.

Occasionally, it is possible to overlook the richness of the world around us. It is easy to entertain only a small range of the full extent of prospects we encounter. Many things may be within our view, but for various reasons we choose to take little notice of them. If we are careful, items in plain sight may be seen afresh and may encourage future inspiration.

Public entry, Creighton University Center for the Arts

Fabrication shop, Gillis Quarries, Ltd.

MILESTONE

MILESTONE

Mass production techniques arrived late in the stone industry. New tools and machines, developed during the industrial revolution, gave entrepreneurs at the start of the twentieth century the ability to transform the manufacturing trades. Mechanization allowed for considerable labor-cost savings and reduced the number of hours it took to process a finished piece of stone. But it wasn't until the 1960s that the stone industry fully embraced Henry Ford's two basic production principles: make standard, interchangeable parts, and assemble them with a minimum of handicraft labor.

The stone industry has had to live up to these principles because, like other areas of commerce at the end of the twentieth century, it came under the influence of the global marketplace. To contend with these conditions, it had to specialize, to continue replacing muscle with machines, and to renew

investment in operations. The latest improvements in stone-processing equipment whittle away at production costs and reduce material waste with little impact on the quality of the final product. As equipment becomes ever more sophisticated, less finishing work is accomplished by hand. Today, many fabricators, instead of working as craftsmen, are now dealers in the material, marketing wares from an increasing number of sources. A greater variety of stone from locations around the world is now available, though the selection of affordable sizes and shapes is more limited. Thin-cut stone is today's common product; it is readily obtainable, reasonably priced and it can be delivered quickly almost anywhere.

In Roman times, hundreds of tons of stone were exported to meet demands from abroad. Today, dispatching stone worldwide has taken on unprecedented magnitude. With the new global marketplace, it is often the case that stone blocks are quarried on one continent, cut and fabricated on another, and installed on a third. Europe's two most active ports of entry for stone—Carrara, Italy, and Antwerp, Belgium— each handle more than 300,000 tons of stone blocks a year[1]. The sources of granite, in the order of importance at these ports are: India, South Africa and Brazil. All of this material leaves the European ports as slabs, processed material, or in original block form. Material movement is increasing at an exponential rate because the cost of fuel, transportation and labor in these distant places of origin is minimal compared to other expenses involved in making new buildings.

Installation preparation, San Angelo Museum of Fine Arts

Although architects, owners, and contractors may benefit from this exchange at this moment, the economic and cultural climate that makes it possible may not last beyond the current era. Moreover, fabricating and installing material away from its place of origin diminishes the intrinsic value of the end product. A stone's geographic starting point, whether it is in Brazil or around the corner, is still important for rooting a building to its surroundings.

Looking out the window of an airplane as it flew low across Vermont a few years ago, I was surprised to see numerous abandoned stone quarries; almost every fifth mountain seemed to have a pit on its slopes. Most date from the early 1800s when large tracts of land were being cleared for farming and towns and villages were springing up to support commerce. They were left behind when the population moved west in search of easier land to cultivate and a better life. In fact, there are deserted stone operations in almost every region of the country, with enough usable material to serve America's stone needs far into the future. They are a magnificent resource, with potential to benefit not only regional architecture but also the environment. In the course of the last 15 years, a New York fabricator I know has returned to four previously abandoned sites.

The material processed from these locations was economic and in close proximity to the constructed buildings.

Environmental advancements are being implemented in the stone industry, namely the introduction of equipment that minimizes waste and spoil piles, the reduction in the amount of energy needed to produce a finished piece of building material and the re-opening of abandoned quarries. The average cost to quarry a ton of stone, including differences in yield for various operations ranges from $50 to $200 a ton[2]. By comparison, the cost of one cubic yard (one and a half tons) of concrete priced by a New York distributor is $63.50[3]; one ton of flat glass is $300[4]; one ton of aluminum, priced on the London Metal Exchange, is $1569[5]; and one ton of acrylic is $1600[6]. In comparison to other products, stone has a modest initial preparation cost, reflecting availability and the minimal amount of energy needed to bring it to the start of the fabrication process.

Many factors contribute to the suitability of a building material for a project and its effect on the environment. Determining a material's degree of sustainability is an elusive task, partly because there is no standard measurement from one type of product to the next and each

Limestone and brick façade detail, Creighton University Center for the Arts

Limestone lobby portal, Creighton University Center for the Arts

Marble addition with existing granite structure, Chatham-Effingham-Liberty Regional Library

individual element of a building should be evaluated with all the others that make a final structure. Even so, if continued care is given to stone's fabrication, handling, and installation, it could be among the group of materials that play a role in sustainable development since it is one that offers the opportunity to create environmentally sound and resource efficient buildings. Achieving structures supportive to the environment that use available materials efficiently is an emerging national goal, and many architects acknowledge the merit of a judicious process for selecting building products. Stone could be high on the list of environmentally appropriate choices if its application were well-considered.

The economics for using stone is customarily evaluated in relation to the longevity of the building it encloses. The life expectancy of stone is at least 100 years, whereas many of the buildings financed and developed during the last four decades were built to last for only one or two generations. Stone was considered a luxury and precluded from use on these projects because the expense of quarrying, cutting, finishing, transporting and installing it was prohibitive compared to the short anticipated life span of these

buildings. Some governmental and civic structures, planned for lengthy occupancy, were the only buildings worthy of the use of the material.

For the last decade, the early obsolescence of buildings has come under close scrutiny because of heightened public and government interest in conserving environmental resources and preserving older structures. A greater number of century-old buildings are occupied today than at any time in our nation's history. All indications are that this phenomenon will continue; more old buildings are being used for a variety of purposes, other than originally intended, in every part of the country.

With longer life expectancies for buildings, stone could be regarded as a less expensive product in terms of economic development, one that plays a complementary role in safeguarding the environment and as a material needing minimal long-term maintenance. Buildings are a monetary and environmental investment. The relationship of the initial cost to the long-term value of a building can be enhanced when durable materials are used for construction. An old structure will qualify economically for reuse when at least 25 percent of its existing value is equivalent to new

Marble façade detail, Chatham-Effingham-Liberty Regional Library capital outlays for construction. Not only does the value of a building increase when durable materials are used, but keeping an older building in use can add to its worth beyond the combined initial outlay and maintenance costs. Changing attitudes about the life span of buildings, including financing and sustainable materials, could dramatically affect the utilization of stone.

1   "Block Imports and Block Storage." Stone. Jan. 2000
2   Various American Suppliers
3   Saunders Concrete Co., Inc., March 24, 2000.
4   A major American Manufacturer
5   London Metal Exchange. 3 Aug. 2000
    http://www.lme.co.uk/data_prices/daily_prices.asp
6   "Resin Pricing." Plastics Technology. Aug. 2000
    http://www.plasticstechnology.com/

Minnesota stone wall and chimney, Highland House

Sandstone, glass and slate façade, Whitaker Center for Science and the Arts

oby, Whitaker Center for Science and the Arts

Patterned slate lobby areas, Whitaker Center for Science and the Arts

Terrace and bay windows, University of the South McClurg Hall

Servery, University of the South McClurg Hall

CORNERSTONE

Detail of historic bankrun stone façade, Western New York State

CORNERSTONE

Before the 1950s, patronage of regional materials gave portions of America unmistakable architectural character. Building products, including stone, were used in particularized ways that corresponded to the specific characteristics of the material and local climatic conditions, thereby giving visual integrity to each locale.

Residents of western New York State, for example, collected rounded rocks from streams and rivers, choosing them for their uniformity of size and shape without regard to color. Placed in evenly spaced rows, these rocks, imbedded in mortar, made walls that covered entire house façades and an occasional church or school. Though these structures seem like rustic poetry now, in the decades from 1800 to 1840 they represented local ingenuity and economy.

Once commonplace, this regionalism is now unfamiliar. The era of economic prosperity following the Second World War introduced a new, homogeneous, popular architecture to every place in our country, from Midland, Texas, to Minneapolis, Minnesota. Simultaneously, the rise of big national business conglomerates and their vast consumer-goods distribution networks all but put "mom-and-pop" enterprises out of existence. Moreover, the new architecture and anonymous corporate parks have made communities virtually indistinguishable from one end of the country to the other. Downtowns, the strips from the airport to the motel and malls now look the same. Large, nondescript horizontal buildings, with gridded, mediocre-abstract, or revival-style mega-architecture, stretch across the landscape. They have generated a new type of environment that consists of huge parking lots surrounding structures with exaggerated details to be seen from cars speeding along highways. Giant illuminated signs point the way. An unanticipated result of this onslaught was the near total demise of regional architecture. Earlier regional enclaves remain, but few, if any, have expanded.

My architectural practice converges around the design of public buildings—auditoriums, libraries, museums and educational facilities—most of them in highly developed areas, such as urban centers, thriving neighborhoods, and educational campuses. These places tend to stand out visually even more as America becomes increasingly uniform. I am convinced that new buildings designed for this type of setting should be endowed with the spirit of the place in which they are constructed. Two challenges confront the designer in adding a new structure to one of these surviving environments. The first is to enhance existing conditions,

Minnesota limestone quarry blocks, Mankato, Minnesota

not diminish them. The second is to find and identify the subtle threads in the local traditions that can be kept alive and advanced.

Architecture is most often conceived and later observed from two divergent vantage points. From a distance, a comprehensive view provides an image and profile for a project that connects it to its surroundings. Up close, the surfaces people come in contact with provide a sense of beauty, utility or both. All new building projects should strive for distinction on both levels.

Every architectural commission in my office is unique, even if it is for a building type I have previously designed. New clients most frequently arrive with specific criteria and performance expectations, that is, size, cost, function and program. Usually, they do not request a "beautiful" building or one with specific imagery. In fact, clients are not inclined to discuss aesthetics, building technology, or construction methods. This is the architect's job.

A client rarely requests the design of a building in a specific material, even though they have requirements for many other parts of their project. In a time when the use of regional materials has been marginalized, I believe they should be reconsidered for their associations with a project's locale and area traditions. Timber, stone, and brick, with obvious regional characteristics, can unite the past and present, and usually have the added benefit of being inexpensive. They can also help root a project in its surrounding community, even when the style and form of the buildings they clad do not replicate older structures.

Many stone purveyors are still small, privately owned businesses located just outside the central part of their communities. There is no explicit way of finding them, but it is not hard to do. In fact, searching out the source of a product is one of the delights of having new work in many areas of the country. Being prepared for the unexpected is a necessity.

One such quest took place in America's heartland, prompted by my firm's work on Orchestra Hall in downtown Minneapolis, which was finished in 1974. Six years later, Tom Doar, the owner of an adjacent parcel of land and Midwest Communications' chairman, called to say he was contemplating a new television broadcast and studio facility for WCCO, a highly successful CBS affiliate. He had considered following its competing stations to the suburbs, but decided to remain in the heart of the city, where the station had originated. He

Fossil lintel and base blocks, WCCO Television Communications Center

had three goals: construct a technologically advanced facility, make a physical contribution to downtown, and create a building reflecting its time.

An open and deliberate planning process with station employees ensued. A year later it resulted in a program, the establishment of technical criteria, a design scheme and budget. Part of the design was based on using local resources, chief among them Minnesota stone, and locally fabricated copper shingles to complement the stone.

I was convinced that this limestone would resonate with the community, not only because it was familiar, but also because it could contrast symbolically with the prominent rooftop display of broadcast equipment. For more than a century, quarries southwest of the Twin Cities provided stone for everything from railroad trestles to buildings. A fine example, and the one I admire most, is the Farmers and Mechanics Bank dating from 1942 in downtown Minneapolis. Its honed Minnesota stone displays the full color range of the material, and contrasts with the stylish art deco detailing and black marble features.

Since little information about the product was available, I had several telephone conversations with the Vetter Stone Company, the largest supplier of the material. During the development of the initial design, we exchanged drawings, material samples and technical data. Late on a Saturday afternoon I made the first of many visits to the Vetter stone operation. Willard, Howard, Walter, Paul Jr and their father started their own company in 1954—almost 70 years after their grandfather, Bernhard, a skilled stonecutter, migrated from his native Germany. On that day, Willard introduced me to their quarrying and fabrication processes. I saw stone being removed from a ledge of material about four feet high, whose color variations were determined by the specific location and the processing method. When the stone was cut parallel to the limestone layers, the color was relatively consistent but when cut perpendicular to the layering, it produced the range of color I admired at the downtown bank building. Willard also pointed out the layer of plant fossils— normally discarded—embedded in the top of the ledge. With information secured from this visit, the final design for the building took its finished form.

The completed WCCO headquarters is a diminutive structure surrounded by much taller and bulkier buildings. It holds its own by sitting sturdily on a two-course base of fossilized stone. Rising from the base to the top of its short, three-

Fossil, honed, rockface and tooled stone finishes, WCCO Television Communications Center

Minnesota limestone facades, WCCO Television Communications Center

Rooftop broadcast equipment, WCCO Television Communications Center

story tower are alternating bands of 30-inch-high, variegated, warm-hued, honed blocks contrasting with eight-inch-high rockfaced courses. Above the main entry and major window openings, at the corner of Nicollet and Eleventh Street, are large fossil-encrusted lintels, the longest of which stretches more than 18 feet. Just before quarrying these stones, the Vetters told me this lintel would be the

largest fabricated in many decades, and would require finding a place in the ledge from which a block this size could be cut in its entirety. The work was undertaken with great care, but even so, I was astonished during my next visit to find that —concerned about possible damage during handling and erection—the Vetters had fabricated not one, but two, 20-ton lintels.

Stone and copper juncture, WCCO Television Communications Center

Stone and copper juncture, WCCO Television Communications Center

Nicollet Avenue facade, WCCO Television Communications Center

With the recent transfer of the business to the Vetter's next generation, there has been no reduction in the effort and concern given to making finished buildings. Equally appreciated by the architect is their ongoing introduction of new equipment, such as water-jet cutting systems and a five-axis routing machine, which adds to the sophistication of their fabrication methods. Because of the Vetters' high-quality work, my firm has used their stone in a number of subsequent projects.

Another search for regional stone took place in west Texas, where, in 1995, I had been selected to design a new downtown art museum for San Angelo, a small city spanning the banks of the Concho River. While defining the program and project cost, the museum director, Howard Taylor, mentioned a stone fabricator that was rumored to have started business about 60 miles northwest of the city. After a number of unsuccessful inquiries, my office was able to locate this operation by telephone, in the small town of Garden City. During the next design meeting in Texas, a half-day exploratory trip was organized for the design team to investigate this stone operation. The two-hour drive through the arid, under-populated landscape allowed us to speculate about what we might discover. Even so, it did not properly prepare us. Garden City, little more

than an intersection, is on the road running west toward Midland. We had been instructed to turn at an historic jail building,—it was the only clue that stone had been used as a building product in this part of Texas—and to drive three miles north to the quarry. There, on the crest of a hill, was a large metal shed with enormous painted letters: TexaStone Quarries. A short distance up their dirt road was a pair of pink stone gateposts. The owners, Connie and Brenda Edwards, and their dog, Bud, gave us the full west Texas welcome: a tour of the fabrication shop (the metal building we had seen from the road) and the showroom, and a walk around the yard, piled high with various pieces of processed stone. During the visit, we saw a large quantity of discarded quarry block "skins," that were naturally deformed, discolored, and highly irregular. We also inspected all the open pits to see the color of the stone being extracted.

By the time we completed the tour and returned to the fabrication shop, it was almost dark. We liked a lot of the material and had numerous questions about its use. To us, the most interesting stones were the discarded quarry block skins. This highly irregular layer of material came from the upper boundary of the limestone deposit, which for millennia had recorded disturbances from erosion, meteors

Historic limestone jail, Garden City, Texas

and other acts of nature. At the end of our visit to Garden
City, everyone agreed a west Texas stone for the museum
had been identified.

A few months later, after developing the design, I returned
to the quarry to examine the material more closely and to
discuss an initial mock-up of a few stone blocks. Four four-

by-eight-foot skins were erected with a series of one-foot,
sawn pieces between them. This demonstration was
important, because the museum director could see for the
first time how the blocks might come together, and it
allowed the architect and fabricator to discuss the technical
requirements of using blocks of this proportion. Since San
Angelo was only two hours away, transportation of finished
pieces this size posed little difficulty.

Limestone quarry block skins mock-up, San Angelo Museum of Fine Arts

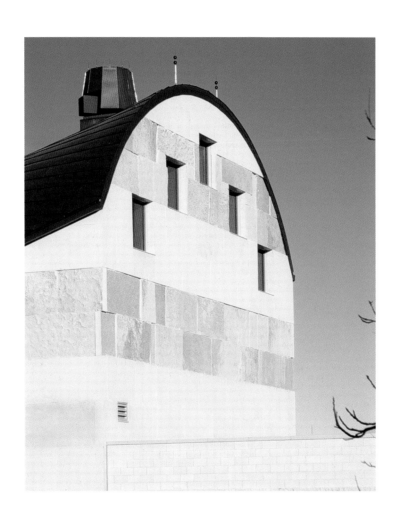

Limestone from block skins and cut pieces, San Angelo Museum of Fine Arts

Façade along North Concho River, San Angelo Museum of Fine Arts

Paseo de Santa Angela façade, San Angelo Museum of Fine Arts

Copper roof and wall, San Angelo Museum of Fine Arts

Stone wall and mesquite floor, San Angelo Museum of Fine Arts

Limestone quarry blocks, Spring Garden, Texas

Proposing the large deformed stone skins for the museum's exterior generated considerable interest from the building committee and elicited requests from them to see the mock-up. When we next arrived in Garden City with this expanded group, instead of the mock-up we were anticipating, we found a full-scale installation cladding one whole side of the metal fabrication shed. The building committee was

unanimous in approving the material and its appearance. Doing business with Connie Edwards has proven to be full of surprises, but they are the kind that propel work forward.

Almost equidistant from Minneapolis and San Angelo, another type of encounter with regional stone awaited me. In 1996, I was selected to design a new dining facility for the University of the South, in Sewanee, Tennessee. Better known simply as "Sewanee," this venerable 150-year-old

Detail of limestone skins and cut pieces, San Angelo Museum of Fine Arts

West entrance, San Angelo Museum of Fine Arts

Sandstone wing wall with limestone finials and slate roof, University of the South McClurg Hall

institution sits on the Cumberland Plateau, 30 miles northwest of Chattanooga. Its first structures were modest wooden buildings, but as the university grew, numerous gothic-inspired structures were made with sandstone quarried on campus. Since the late nineteenth century, this material has been used for everything from fireplaces to ashlar walls. In the 1950s the university acquired a stone saw to speed fabrication of building blocks. A decade later the quarries were closed and large quantities of stone, when needed, were purchased from suppliers in the region.

For 20 years, Houston King has been a part of the Physical Plant Services Department, which oversees the operations and maintenance of the existing buildings and new construction. For the last decade, he has been the university stonemason. Following a design review meeting with faculty, students, and other individuals interested in the project, Houston asked me about the possibility of using stone from the campus for the new dining hall. This was an unexpected proposition, as I knew stone in any quantity had not been available for at least 20 years, except for modest repairs to existing structures. From his inquiry came a new building that is clad in 750 tons of sandstone from the reopened campus quarries and a sizable amount from other nearby sources. All but 300 tons of the material, excluding the decorative limestone finials, was fabricated on campus. Getting from a dozen pieces of sandstone mocked up for review by the university regents to a completed structure in four years' time was an intricate process. Although stone was available and could be fabricated on campus, finding professional masons was difficult in this remote location. Competitive pricing for installation was finally achieved by inviting masonry contractors from outside the region to participate.

The most compelling aspect of this remarkable enterprise was the university community's unflagging interest in reviving the use of sandstone from their campus for a major project. The dining hall, in making visual and physical reference to Sewanee's most revered buildings, could not have paid such stunning homage to this educational institution's heritage with any other material.

Standstone, flashing, and curtain wall mock-up, University of the South McClurg Hall

Refectory dining niches, University of the South McClurg Hall

Refectory, University of the South McClurg Hall

Limestone tower and metal roof, University of Nebraska at Omaha Fine Arts Building

QUARRY STONE

QUARRY STONE

To use stone effectively today requires research about the material. This is an exploratory and analytic activity. Selecting a specific stone, determining appropriate finishes, evaluating methods of erection, and assessing potential design ideas commence with understanding the resources available at the quarry. Stone's fabrication and the architecture that results have changed just as stone has evolved from a product of nature to one of commerce. But even in this new millennium, as fabricators and suppliers adjust to an expanding global economy, both the manufacture of stone products and the practice of architecture retain elements of their cottage-industry origins. Devotion to craft, work performed by groups of similarly inclined people, modest return on initial investment, and a personal vision are still at the heart of these two endeavors.

Every stone contains traces of its evolution. The quarry is where its potential as a building material can be fully appreciated. Here, one can best determine whether to apply it in conventional or uncommon ways and whether the finished results will be ordinary or aspire to the lyrical. I derive as much information from quarry visits as from any other factor affecting design.

Some types of stone are infinitely malleable; others are not because of constraints most easily understood at the source. Visits to quarries are an integral part of my working method and usually occur in the early stages of a building's design. Occasionally, I tour a quarry simply to push my thinking in a divergent direction. No matter what the circumstances, these excursions inevitably inspire new ideas, provide moments of conjecture, or prompt reappraisal of information previously gathered.

During a 1999 visit to Scotland, Ian Begg—a friend and architect—suggested I travel with him to Caithness, in the northeastern section of the mainland, whose slate has been well-known for centuries. A visit to the same region 25 years earlier had left me with an indelible image of long rows of thin slate slabs securely positioned on end to form fences that separated fields. Roofing flags and paving blocks from this area of Scotland were world-famous from 1800 to 1920, but are no longer in demand outside the country, because of more recently developed sources for the material.

Ian invited me to return to Caithness to meet Jack Green, the owner and operator of the Halkirk Quarry—a two-person operation. During this visit, I learned that Jack had started there as a teenager in 1930; he still labors in much the same way he did 70 years ago. In fact, his work method is not very different from what it would have been 500 years ago. His simple tools—two hammers of different sizes, steel wedges, and a crowbar—extract thick slabs that will become paving blocks, hearths, or countertops, and thinner sheets for roofing slates. After Jack advances with the wedge and

hammer into the deposit's horizontal layers, he pries up a piece of stone with a short rod. Because he has been at this so long, he instantly decides whether or not the loosened material is viable. Pieces are put aside for later shaping. The thick material is cut to the desired size with a homemade device that looks like a cross between a lawnmower and a carpet sweeper, with a blade attached. The roofing slates are

Roofing slates, Caithness, Scotland

shaped by scratching a rectangular outline on a selected piece, balancing it on a rod and chopping it along the line with a slater's knife. A skilled worker can produce 12 to 15 slates in an hour. Because of its simple, age-old methods, this operation seems like a thing of the past, but so does the commodity they are producing.

Since my first visit to Caithness I've speculated about the source of the nineteenth century slate sidewalk around the corner from my office at 20th Street and Broadway. Could it have originated from a quarry operation similar to Jack Green's? Whether boat ballast or a special shipment, we may never be certain of the events that brought these stone

Jack Green in quarry

slabs to New York City. What we do know, however, is that between nature and people such as Jack, this material can assume many durable shapes and forms.

One of the places I associate with stone is Vermont. Two building projects at Middlebury College allowed me to get acquainted with this state's most familiar stones, marble and granite. In 1985 I began the design process for a pair of projects on this pastoral campus. My favorite buildings constructed during this college's 200-year history were the original row of three structures. These are tall, narrow, straightforward buildings made with available stone of varying size, laid up in a random pattern. From a distance they look more like mill buildings than places for education. Over the years they were used for purposes that necessitated interior changes, but their exteriors remain as robust and striking as the day they were built.

These original structures provoked a quick tour of the state's stone operations. It was soon apparent that no standard products from these sources would conform to Middlebury's $150-per-square-foot building budget. After looking at the normal stock, I examined non-building pieces for possible use. One alternative was stone produced for a federal government order: marble gravesite monuments. These two-inch thick slabs with rounded tops had potential as repetitive wall units or special accent pieces, but the fixed dimensions and shape did not prove to be workable.

Another large Vermont supplier had numerous standard granite products from which to choose but none of these were within our budget either. During the tour of their operations I saw discarded quarry block skins in the spoil pile. A discussion ensued about using these, since they seemed affordable. After careful consideration, this supplier understood the seriousness of my desire to use this scrap material. Unfortunately, they decided the price for this stone would be no different from that of standard products. There would be no discount for using their usually worthless material.

Unfortunately, quarry visits are not always productive. Occasionally they result in the expenditure of time and effort without finding serviceable products. This lack of success in Vermont led to nearby quarries in Massachusetts and Quebec. The two Middlebury buildings were constructed for the budget using granite: red blocks 23 inches high, and gray blocks 18 inches high. The gray granite blocks were taken from an ordinary run of

Croft ruin, North Uist, Scotland

Granite entry tower and theater with copper roof, Middlebury College Center for the Arts

street curbing material. Their sawn top and bottom faces allowed for even wall courses. The split surfaces; front, back and ends, were irregular and granite 'chinks' were used to minimize the amount of mortar between blocks to fill the larger than normal vertical joints. The remainder of the building was sheathed in two frequently used regional materials, wood clapboards and roofing slates.

In the expectation of matching stone for the Cleveland Public Library's new Louis Stokes Wing to that of its 1928 predecessor, I visited its source, the century-old quarry in Tate, Georgia. Because stone had been extracted continuously from the same quarry pit for 70 years, there was uncertainty about finding comparable material. While a match was the intended purpose of the visit, it was difficult not to witness other aspects of this operation.

Granite clad concert hall, copper shingle roof and dormers, Middlebury College Center for the Arts

During tours of their pits, fabrication shops, and stored marble, I observed a vast array of quarry blocks that had been produced prior to the introduction of saws. The drills used to extract those blocks were so tightly and regularly spaced that the resulting parallel grooves made their exterior surfaces appear fluted. The entry portal to the new Louis Stokes Wing of the library, assembled from the drilled

outer surfaces of the quarry blocks, makes a visual reference to the fluted columns of its neo-classical predecessor. At the time of the original quarry visit, my intention was to determine if a color and veining "match" could be made after so many years of operation. Not only did this prove possible, but I also discovered the flutes that suggest a second link between the new construction and the existing historic structure.

Granite quoins at theater/lobby openings, Middlebury College Center for the Arts

Drilled marble quarry blocks, Tate, Georgia

Drilled marble entry portal with granite lintel

Marble corner towers, Cleveland Public Library, Stokes Wing

Reader and Tom Otterness Sculpture, Cleveland Public Library

Rockwell Avenue façade, Cleveland Public Library, Stokes Wing

Quarry, Gillis Quarries, Ltd.

FREE STONE

FREE STONE

Stone production varies widely, and its application requires that an architect understand the equipment used to manufacture final building units and the methods for installing them. While the removal of material from the mantle of the earth has imperceptibly evolved since the initiation of its use, reliance on the computer is now integral to all aspects of construction. The architect should take into account that finished stone surfaces no longer bear the marks of the stonecutters' virtuosity. Instead, the introduction of technologically advanced machinery has resulted in the almost total demise of hand-cut stone blocks, which in turn has eliminated some types of finishes and detailing. Long gone are the tooled finishes from hand-held chisels that could render differences in texture across the face of a stone block, or from one stone to the next. Now, machine splitting provides rustication, and other equipment makes tooled, honed, rockface, and polished finishes. The results may be unrefined in some instances, but it is possible to achieve subtleties formerly reached exclusively through hand labor.

Machinery for splitting stone can now accommodate pieces measuring several feet on a side and weighing many tons. Stone this size can be sheared with a single blow from a pneumatic multi-blade splitter. The 30-by-64 inch, split face, red granite blocks enclosing the music room and main entry to the Middlebury College Center for the Arts in Vermont were produced by taking advantage of this type of device. Without this kind of equipment, the fabricator would have had to revert to hand work for the same result at many times the cost.

The procedure for cutting and finishing stone is important, because the expense of each piece increases in proportion to its level of refinement, and the number of times it is handled. On numerous occasions, I have found building products requiring neither the highest level of finish, nor the greatest amount of handling. Such lack of refinement often reveals the "making" process (split surfaces, drill, and saw marks), left behind as an imprint. They can be used to considerable effect on a building's surface in much the same way that hand markings were previously. The main entry to the Middlebury College Center for Fine Arts has a portal that incorporates two 64-inch tall square granite quarry blocks with these types of marks. Imprints, from drilling and sawing, plus rough corners, contrast with the surrounding split stone to further distinguish this special place.

Granite blocks at main entry, Middlebury College Center for the Arts

At one time, more than half of all material quarried was discarded during the production of a finished building unit, but, new processing equipment has brought waste down to about 20 percent at some operations. For my projects, I employ stone fabricated in standard ways, pieces made to specific size and finish. I also utilize material not typically sold for buildings. The outer surfaces of quarry blocks are

usually discarded due to their rough appearance (a result of the extraction process), but under certain circumstances, they can become building units. Normally intended for the scrap pile, these pieces are more economical than those cut from the center of the blocks. Since the stone fabrication process begins with the removal of the skins, I often ask fabricators to cut them at a greater than normal thickness to compensate for their irregularity. Suppliers are generally

Granite entryway, Middlebury College Center for the Arts

Cemetary, Queens, New York

agreeable, because, instead of "filleting" out the most desirable portion and discarding the rest, they can utilize the entire block, thus generating income from all the material. This was the method employed at the San Angelo Museum of Fine Arts where the skins form a few horizontal bands and the material's remainder is integrated into the rest of the façade. I seldom work with the least expensive products, but search for ways to achieve the desired design results and the greatest value possible with the available material.

Some fabricators have dual operations, where architectural building units are produced separately from other products. As mass production of thousands of repetitive units is very economical, stone for cemetery monuments or street curbing is considered a different commodity than material destined for building walls. Using such standard-size units for building construction instead of their original purpose can yield significant savings. Dakota mahogany granite, initially intended for monument use, served equally well as wall surfacing material at both the Highland House, in Madison,

Wisconsin and the Weber Fine Arts Center, at The University of Nebraska, in Omaha.

Ironically, a novel way for erecting walls similar to the centuries-old dry-set stone method has evolved in the last few decades. It allows wind and precipitation to penetrate an open gap between stone blocks. The elements, rather than being repelled at the exterior face of the building, move past it toward an interior water and wind proof surface beyond. First used on outdoor roofdecks with habitable spaces below, this technique has been turned on end and is now a popular method of wall construction. After application to high-rise buildings, it now appears on low-rise structures too. From a distance, a building employing this method of construction may look as though its blocks have mortar between them. Up close, though, one will find that a continuous opening, generally not more than an inch, surrounds the edge of each stone block. (Most observers are unaware that concealed hardware, normally stainless steel, provides the physical attachment to the building structure.) Material installed in this way looks

North façade, Highland House

North façade, Highland House

weightless and thin, appearing to defy gravity. The effect is cartoonish, almost as if the image has been reversed, because emphasis is shifted from stone to the dark gap that surrounds it. Though in some instances this method achieves economy of construction, it no longer acknowledges gravity—one of the properties I value most about stone.

Stone details, Highland House

View to Shepard Tower from meeting room, University of the South McClurg Hall

Fabrication shop, Gillis Quarries, Ltd.

141

Superior Avenue façade, Cleveland Public Library, Stokes Wing

KEYSTONE

Oval and corner tower model pieces, Cleveland Public Library, Stokes Wing

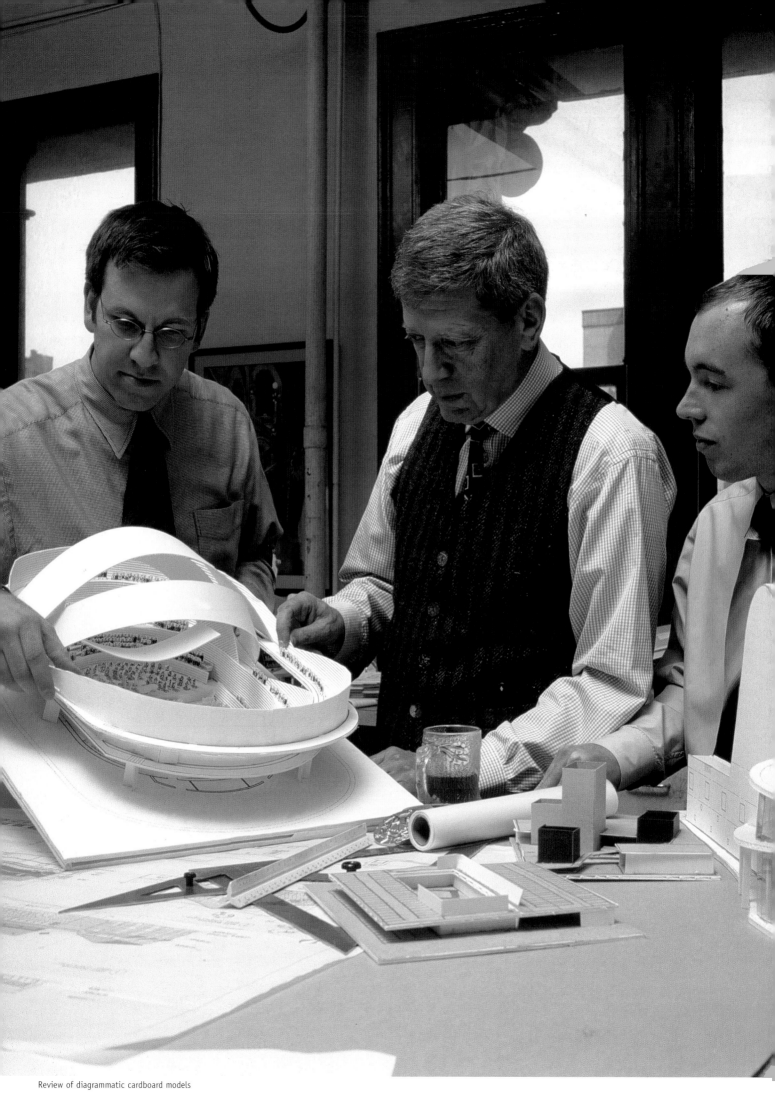

Review of diagrammatic cardboard models

KEYSTONE

Early in my internship as an architect I realized being passionate about this calling was not enough; it would require being resourceful and industrious. To achieve design distinction would necessitate exploring every aspect of the profession—a lifelong pursuit.

I have grown, for instance, to respect the incongruity between design conception and execution, initial ideas and built form, renderings and completed building. Many architects prefer one to the other, choosing between the gritty vitality of the building process or the considerations of design and theory. Resolving this polarity is of paramount importance in my work, where I endeavor to manifest abstract ideas in the buildings and to create impressions of the physical in the abstract designs. Keeping the two intertwined is the challenge.

Buildings naturally find expression from materials; in a less straightforward way giving form to a theory can have an equivalent result. It is only in the diligent development of the use of materials and ideas that exemplary architecture occurs; one without the other will not suffice. There can be exhilaration in architecture but there can also be tedium. Proceeding from the intangible to the tangible is a lengthy but ordered sequence, tailored to each project.

The initiation of a new commission usually begins with the creation of a series of concept models, which determine the nature of the design challenge ahead. Progressing from one idea to the next in an incremental, but not necessarily linear way, transforms concepts into actual forms (albeit paper, glue, and cardboard). Utilized not for client presentations but to generate dialogue about design considerations, the models give shape to what is in my mind's eye and make the imagined explicit enough to stimulate discussion among the small group of individuals working on a project with me. Additions and subtractions occur frequently. These models embody thoughts about generating a building's forms: their arrangement, relationship to the ground, and organization. They also initiate conversations about structure and materials.

Brilliant as design ideas may be, they require considerable advancement before they are realized in built form. Three distinct, but interdependent tasks—specifications, drawings, and research—are developed simultaneously to sustain the constantly evolving design. Written specifications describe the criteria for materials as well as the means and methods for putting them together. Drawings graphically delineate the desired result. Computer technology has altered the process of

---

1/2" to the foot plexiglass and cardboard model, Cleveland Public Library, Stokes Wing

making both but has not changed their content.

In illustrating complex shapes, intricate forms and complicated dimensions, the computer is indispensable. But to arrive at these two recording tasks, the architect must concurrently undertake the most ambiguous and arduous job: research on materials. Understanding the characteristics of a material requires extensive fieldwork (normally quarry

visits for stone) at the outset of a project. The importance of this kind of analysis is not always apparent to the observer of a completed building.

Manufacturers' literature and sales representatives can provide data about their stones' strength, rate of water absorption, cost and availability. But little can be learned about less tangible qualities from the two-inch-by-two-inch

Detail of bluestone base building, Rainbow Bridge U.S. Customs and Immigration Center

View from Canada, Rainbow Bridge U.S. Customs and Immigration Center

Minnesota stone, terra cotta, and glass-block façade, Los Angeles County Museum of Art Anderson Building

samples usually provided to architects in their offices. To appreciate a stone's full color range, the potential for specific detailing, or its ability to catch light and shade on its finished surfaces requires a careful examination of the product at its source. Taking the time to visit quarry operations and inspect the materials and fabrication processes yields reliable information to guide its ultimate use. No two classifications of igneous, metamorphic, or sedimentary stone are the same. Nor are natural materials uniform, so one must be intimately familiar with their physical properties: consistencies, blemishes, randomness of pattern and color.

During visits to fabrication shops, I often have a series of stones erected to simulate a wall surface. This demonstration is not simply an exercise about technical considerations but more importantly may suggest ways to go about achieving the desired final results. This wall, even without the benefit of mortar, accurate block size, or adjoining materials, allows me to envision the final installation and to decide whether or not it will be acceptable. If the mock-up is not satisfactory, changes can be immediately made and the process can move forward.

My office employs conventional illustrations to document stone construction: sections, details and elevations of all wall surfaces. In addition, at least one drawing portrays an inventory of every type of stone used in the project, with each piece depicted isometrically to show volume. This diagram provides dimensions, angles for straight cuts, radius points and other pertinent information. As soon as the contractor submits shop drawings for fabrication approval, all building units are reviewed again for design conformance and constructability.

Specifications—drawings' verbal counterparts—present those elements of a building that cannot easily be drawn. The method of attaching stone blocks to each other and to a building structure is outlined here. Centuries ago, mortar between blocks of stone was considered preferable, because it kept the wind and water out and allowed the building's interior to be used to greater advantage. As a method of construction, it superseded dry-set placement of stone, where no mortar was used between building units. The course of action for accomplishing the erection of stonewalls is delineated in the specifications.

Fabricated pieces waiting installation, Sewanee, Tennessee

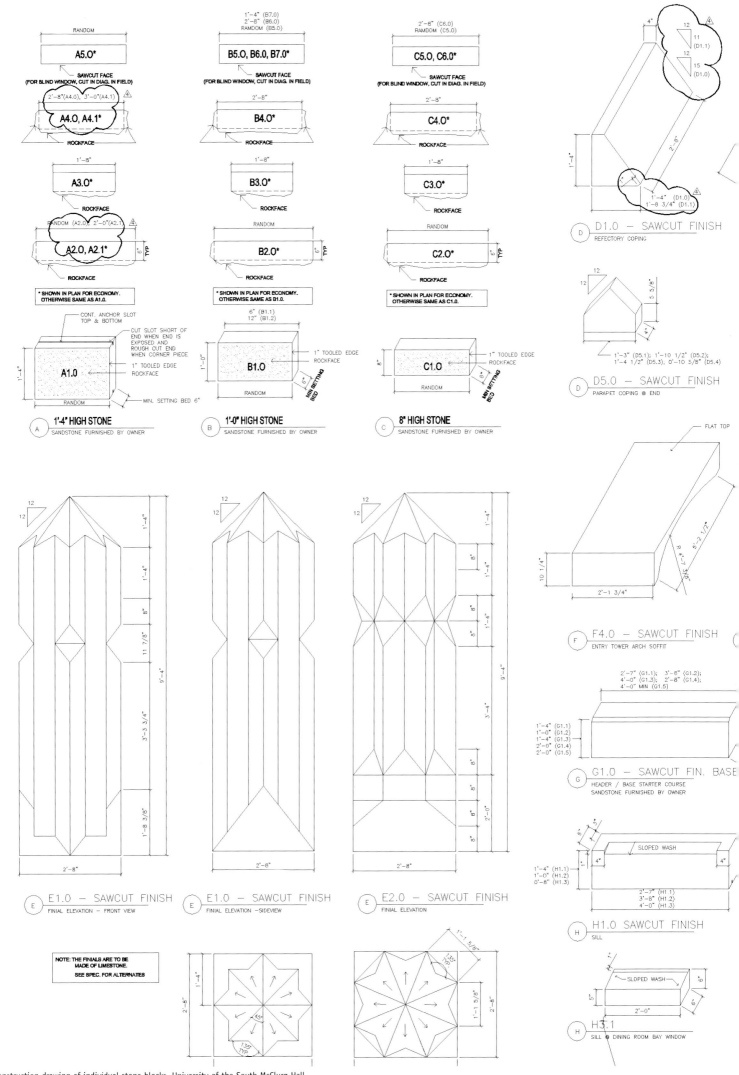

Construction drawing of individual stone blocks, University of the South McClurg Hall

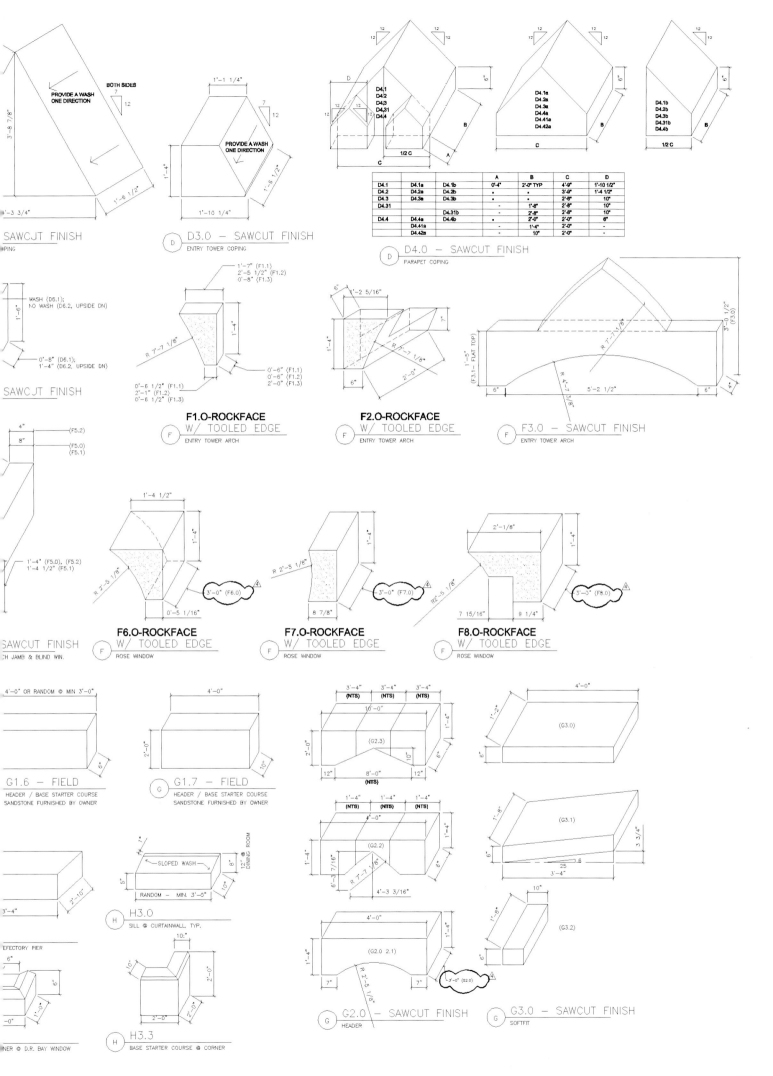

			A	B	C	D
D4.1	D4.1a	D4.1b	0'-4"	2'-0" TYP	4'-9"	1'-10 1/2"
D4.2	D4.2a	D4.2b	"	"	3'-9"	1'-4 1/2"
D4.3	D4.3a	D4.3b	"	"	2'-8"	10"
D4.31			-	1'-8"	2'-8"	10"
		D4.31b	-	2'-8"	2'-8"	10"
D4.4	D4.4a	D4.4b	"	2'-0"	2'-0"	6"
	D4.41a		-	1'-4"	2'-0"	-
	D4.42a		-	10"	2'-0"	-

The setting in place of stone at the construction site is as important as its selection and documentation. Thorough as construction and specification documents can be, architects should take special care to insure that intentions stated at the outset of a project are realized in the final structure. Determining the acceptability of the final installation prior to the start of construction is a necessity in achieving the

desired results. Preparation of the stone (its cutting and finish), the mortar, the placement of all building materials together, their structural integrity, and relationship to other building elements should be reviewed in a mock-up (a small portion of the building made full scale). The erection of a wall section, no bigger than 10 by 20 feet, before construction starts has become a requirement of all my building projects. This confirms the mason's ability to install

Stone mock-up, WCCO Television Communications Center

Entrance to Times Mirror Central Court, Los Angeles County Museum of Art

Wilshire Boulevard façade, Los Angeles County Museum of Art, Anderson Building

the stone as described in the construction documents. It also allows the architect and contractor to anticipate specific topics that might arise during construction, such as lippage between blocks, shape and color of mortar joints, methods for locating unusually colored or marked stone pieces, dimensions between stones, and transition between materials. More important, the mock-up serves as a standard

for acceptable work and permits discussion of anticipated construction conditions, thus avoiding delays once work is underway. This process provides the client a chance to view a full-size simulation of the finished building. Drawings and a small stone sample are not always adequate for conveying design intent or desired results to non-architects. I do not let a building go into construction unless it has the very best efforts, careful attention and approval of all involved parties.

Minnesota stone, terra cota, and glass block entry portal, Los Angeles County Museum of Art, Anderson Building

The design process is carried forward by vigorously examining the criteria for material selection, attaining value for each dollar spent, and determining the means of construction. It includes office-based efforts to verbally and visually describe the building project and the fieldwork to locate materials, approve methods for their use, and verify that construction conforms to the design. The integration of

these distinct types of work insures that the bits of data gathered over many months are distilled and incorporated into the constructed building.

Acute corner detail, Los Angeles County Museum of Art, Anderson Building

Bullnose, sawn, tooled and rusticated blocks, Virginia Museum of Fine Arts, West Wing

BRIMSTONE

BRIMSTONE

Stone is just one of many products that might be considered for a building project. Even with a strong passion for the material, an architect must have good reason to select it. Rather than rate building materials on a predetermined scale of good to bad or genuine to ersatz, I choose them for their inherent virtues, ease of application and value. A material's real worth is not its cost, but its ability to invoke the architect's intended design.

The method I use for the orderly development of a project considers various tasks simultaneously. Speculation, curiosity and inquiry accompany all facets of the work, from the shaping of forms and spaces for specific uses to identifying materials that will invigorate the design. Imagination is a catalyst—it can speed the thought process. At the outset of a project the focus is not on one material at the expense of others, but on the selection without bias in deference to the best possible realization of the building. My completed buildings employ many materials in various ways: The San Angelo Museum of Fine Arts is entirely clad in stone to magnify the importance of a small but important community cultural building; at the Murchison Center stone serves as a fanciful counterpoint to three other materials enlivening a large composition along an interstate highway; and the Fox Theater is entirely constructed of synthetic parts—stone is not used at all.

When presenting historic buildings, architectural journals and books usually depict cathedrals, palaces and governmental structures made with handcrafted stone blocks. Ordinary stone buildings erected simultaneously alongside these larger-than-life structures are not frequently portrayed. They, too, were built with care and attention but on a modest scale, with less sophisticated material.

View along Paseo de Santa Angela, San Angelo Museum of Fine Arts

Limestone, clay tile and galvanized screening, San Angelo Museum of Fine Arts

Buildings enduring from prior centuries are still contemporaneous. The ideals they impart link the past and the present. These structures are worth understanding and in some instances even emulating. Evocative buildings are packed with physical illustrations and ideas for us to ponder. They indicate a method for making architecture down to the smallest detail.

Designing with stone today often requires utilizing ordinary material in exceptional ways even for projects that aspire to the monumental. This incongruity, that would have been unacceptable a century ago, is now one of the inescapable challenges. The expressive intensity of the material has been there from the beginning of its use and the rich textures, colors and finishes cannot be found in other materials. The history of stone building is an evolutionary story about the progressive assimilation and unification of knowledge and the emergence of common methods for construction.

Because of the current array of products competing for architects' attention, stone can be overlooked as a viable building material. It is common for designers to entertain only a small familiar group of products inside the full spectrum of those available. Some may regard the pursuit of just the right kind of stone for a project as too time-consuming; examining a series of alternatives requires both research and a vision of how to put this natural resource into service.

Giving stone an evocative presence requires a design process without constraint. Uniting the dazzling beauty of this natural material as it comes from the ground with industrial precision and economy necessitates an examination of its limits as well as its possibilities. My objective is to employ simple installations when appropriate and to go beyond them when it is fitting in order to educe more subtle attributes. The choice of stone should relate to the circumstances of the project at hand, and should achieve results not possible with any other product. The challenge to make the most of a material's distinctive qualities is an invitation to advance design. I have found a variety of ways to bring out stone's latent properties to forge forms and mold spaces, to enliven environments with color and texture, and to arouse human interest. Stone's unexpected attributes, properly emphasized, can cast a transforming light on a finished piece of architecture.

Limestone detail, University of North Texas Performing Arts Center

Concert hall, University of North Texas Performing Arts Center

East facade, University of the South McClurg Hall

My interest in materials has been sustained by 30 years of commissions, and my work has been dedicated to discovering, matching, and improving the spirit of these projects. The public practice of architecture requires making buildings while revealing personal ideas and interests. It is imperative for the architect to open up imaginative possibilities that initially might have seemed contrary to reality.

Quarry blocks, Gillis Quarries, Ltd.

APPENDIX

Circulation desk in new atrium

Reading room demising wall

Reader tables

Marble addition

Adult collection clerestory

Chatham-Effingham-Liberty Regional Library

Savannah, Georgia

Stone Type: marble

Cut/Finish: split-face and sawn

Size: 8" high x 4" thick x random lengths (split-face)
4" thick dimensional stone x random lengths (sawn)

Source/Quarrier/Fabricator:
The Georgia Marble Company, Tate, GA

Contractor: Mitchell Construction Company, Inc.

Mason/Installer: M. Garcia & Sons, Inc.

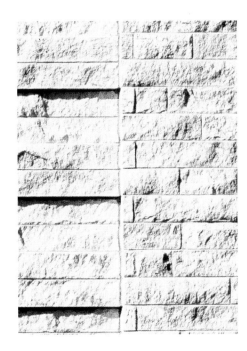

Design Team:
Malcolm Holzman: Partner-in-Charge
Daria Pizzetta: Project Manager
Robert Almodovar: Project Architect
Sally Copeland
Jill Sicinski: Interiors

Associate Architect: Cogdell & Mendrala Architects

Interior corner tower detail

Tile wall at circulation desk

Superior Avenue façade

Eastman Reading Garden

Corner reading room

Louis Stokes Wing, Cleveland Public Library

Cleveland, Ohio

Stone Type 1: marble

Cut/Finish: split-face blocks, fluted quarry block faces and sawn blocks

Size: 8" high x 4"- 6" thick x random lengths (split face)
4' high x 4' thick x 8' long (quarry blocks)
4" thick dimensional stone (sawn)

Source/Quarrier/Fabricator: The Georgia Marble Company, Tate, GA

Stone Sill and Base Detail
1   Reinforced CMU wall
2   Rigid insulation
3   4" thick split-face marble
4   6" thick split-face marble
5   Sawn-face marble sill
6   Sawn-face marble base

Stone Type 2: two granite lintels

Cut/Finish: sawn

Size: 9' high x 16" thick x 30' long, lintel

Source/Quarrier/Fabricator: Rock of Ages, Barre, Vermont

Construction Manager: Turner Construction Company in association with Colejon Construction, Choice Construction, and Ozanne Construction

Mason/Installer: Cleveland Marble Mosaic Company (interior)
Harmon Contract (exterior)

Design Team:
Malcolm Holzman: Partner-in-Charge
Robert Almodovar: Project Manager/ Project Architect
Kala Somvanshi: Project Manager
Setrak Ohannessian: Project Architect
Manuel Mergal
Bruce Spenadel
Rob Lopez
Michael Connolly
Jeff Porten
Kristopher Nikolich
Christopher Bach
Allen Robinson
Victor Rodriguez
Daria Pizzetta: Interiors
Robin Kunz: Interiors
Nancy Geng: Interiors
Susan Pon: Interiors

Associate Architects: URS Greiner
Robert P. Madison International

Art gallery

Dance studio

Façade detail

350-seat auditorium

Lobby

Lied Education Center for the Arts

Creighton University
Omaha, Nebraska

Stone Type: limestone

Cut/Finish: split-face front, back and ends

Size: 8″ high x 4″ thick x random lengths

Source/Quarrier/Fabricator: Gillis Quarries, Ltd, Winnipeg, Manitoba, Canada

Contractor: Kiewitt Construction Company

Mason/Installer: Kehm Contractors

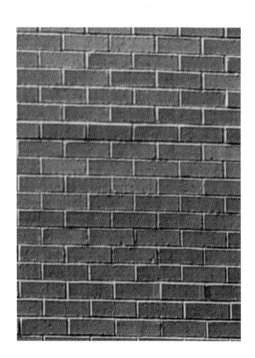

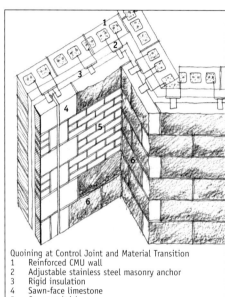

Quoining at Control Joint and Material Transition
1   Reinforced CMU wall
2   Adjustable stainless steel masonry anchor
3   Rigid insulation
4   Sawn-face limestone
5   Common brick
6   Split-face limestone

Design Team:
Malcolm Holzman: Partner-in-Charge
Robert Almodovar: Project Manager/
Project Architect
Nestor Bottino
Michael Connolly
James Brogan
Caroline Bertrand: Interiors

Associate Architect:
The Schemmer Associates

Dining room

Kitchen

Juxtaposition of granite, limestone and metal shingles, Highland House

North façade at night, Highland House

View from meridian to dining room

Highland House

Stone Type 1: limestone

Cut/Finish: split-face

Size: 7-1/2" high x 4" thick x random lengths

Source/Quarrier/Fabricator: Vetter Stone Company, Kasota, MN

Stone Type 2: granite

Cut/Finish: split-face

Size: 7-1/2" high x 4" thick x random lengths

Madison, Wisconsin

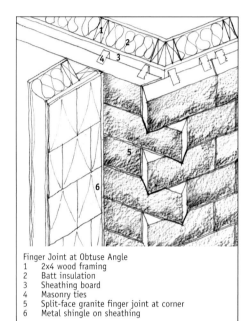

Finger Joint at Obtuse Angle
1 2x4 wood framing
2 Batt insulation
3 Sheathing board
4 Masonry ties
5 Split-face granite finger joint at corner
6 Metal shingle on sheathing

Source/Quarrier/Fabricator: Dakota Granite Company, Milbank, SD

Contractor: Ehlers Construction, Inc.

Design Team:
Malcolm Holzman: Partner-in-Charge
Douglas Moss: Project Manager/
Project Architect
Caroline Bertrand: Interiors

Entry way from Wilshire Boulevard

Entry portal

Minnesota stone, terra cotta, and glass-block façade

Gallery

Gallery stair

Robert O. Anderson Building

Los Angeles County
Museum of Art
Los Angeles, California

Stone Type 1: limestone
Cut/Finish: tapestry finish

Size: 3" thick

Source/Quarrier/Fabricator: Vetter Stone Company, Kasota, MN

Contractor: Turner Construction Company

Mason/Installer: DBM Hatch

Design Team:
Norman Pfeiffer: Partner-in-Charge
Malcolm Holzman: Collaborative Design Partner
Hugh Hardy: Collaborative Design Partner
Stephen Johnson: Project Manager
Harris Feinn: Project Manager
Pamela Loeffelman: Project Architect
Hilda Lowenberg
Setrak Ohannessian
Neil Dixon
Donald Billinkoff
David Gross
David Hoggatt
Candace Renfro
Lindsay Reeds
Charles Muse
Jonathan Strauss
Jack Martin
Mark Tannin
Evan Carzis
Mike McGlone
Susan Olroyd
Dan Lincoln
Robin Kunz: Interiors
Darlene Fridstein: Interiors

Upper level lobby

Art gallery

Entry pavilion

Studio theater

Concert hall

Center for the Arts

Middlebury College
Middlebury, Vermont

Stone Type 1: granite

Cut/Finish: split-face with sawn tops and bottoms, lintels and sills

Size: 16" high x 6" thick x random lengths

Source/Quarrier: Fletcher Granite Co., North Chelmsford, MA

Fabricator: Granite Importers, Barre, VT

Design Team:
Malcolm Holzman: Partner-in-Charge
Robert Almodovar: Project Manager
William Boling
Ben Caldwell
Mark DeMarta
Harris Feinn
Lee Harris
Raoul Lowenberg
Hilda Lowenberg
John Maddox
Manuel Mergal
Gilbert Sanchez
Robin Kunz: Interiors
Diane Lam: Interiors

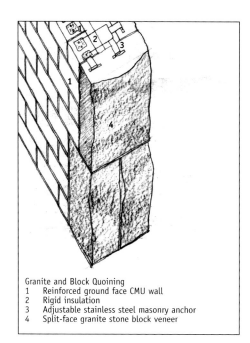

Granite and Block Quoining
1   Reinforced ground face CMU wall
2   Rigid insulation
3   Adjustable stainless steel masonry anchor
4   Split-face granite stone block veneer

Stone Type 2: granite

Cut/Finish: split-face with sawn tops and bottoms, lintels and sills

Size: 2'-8" high x 8"-12" thick x 5'-4" long

Source/Quarrier: Columbia Granite, Tadussac, Quebec, Canada

Fabricator: Granite Importers, Inc., Barre, VT

Contractor/Mason/Installer:
Pizzagalli Construction Co.

McCullough Lounge

McCullough Lounge

Clapboard and granite addition, Middlebury College Student Activities Center

McCullough Lounge

Crest Room

McCullough Student Center

Middlebury College
Middlebury, Vermont

Stone Type 1: granite

Cut/Finish: split-face with sawn tops and bottoms, lintels and sills

Size: 16" high x 8" thick x random lengths

Source/Quarrier: Fletcher Granite Co., North Chelmsford, MA

Fabricator: Granite Importers, Inc., Barre, VT

Contractor/Mason/Installer: Engelberth Construction, Inc.

Design Team:
Malcolm Holzman: Partner-in-Charge
Robert Almodovar: Project Manager
Cleveland Adams
Tracy Aronoff
Ben Caldwell
Raoul Lowenberg
Hilda Lowenberg
Gilbert Sanchez
Douglas Stebbins
Robin Kunz: Interiors
Diane Lam: Interiors

Toll plaza

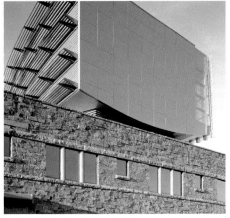

Juncture of bluestone base and bridge

Detail of bluestone base building

West façade

Façade detail

U.S. Customs and Immigration Rainbow Bridge Center

Niagara, New York

Stone Type 1: sandstone (hamilton bluestone)

Cut/Finish: sawed bed, natural cleft and random course ashlars

Size: random

Source: Alcove Quarry

Quarrier/Fabricator: New York Quarries, Inc., Alcove, NY

Contractor: Ciminelli-Cowper Construction Management

Mason/Installer: Alba

Design Team:
Hugh Hardy: Partner-in-Charge
Jack Martin: Project Manager
Maya Schali: Project Architect
Douglas Freeman: Construction Architect
Phillip Klinkon
Yasin Abdullah
Ching-Wen Lin
James Brogan
Ted Sheridan
Amy Wagenbach

Gallery

Gallery

West entrance, San Angelo Museum of Fine Arts

Stone wall and mesquite floor, San Angelo Museum of Fine Arts

Lobby

San Angelo Museum of Fine Arts and Education Center

San Angelo, Texas

Stone Type 1: limestone

Cut/Finish: top of the ledge, bottom of the ledge, sawn, and split-face

Size: 7-5/8" high x 3-1/2" thick x 16" long
4' high x 10" thick x 8' long

Source/Quarrier/Fabricator: TexaStone Quarries, Garden City, TX

Contractor: Templeton Construction

Mason/Installer: Brazos Masonry

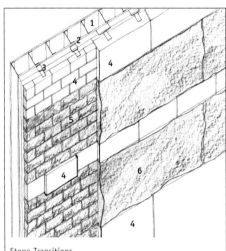

Stone Transitions
1   Structural gauge metal stud wall
2   Sheathing and rigid insulation
3   Adjustable stainless steel masonry anchor
4   Sawn-face limestone
5   Split-face limestone
6   Ledge split-face limestone

Design Team:
Malcolm Holzman: Partner-in-Charge
Douglas Moss: Project Manager/ Project Architect
Nestor Bottino: Project Advisor
Chris Kaiser: Construction Architect
Michael Connolly
Yasin Abdullah
Maya Schali
Winslow Wu
Steven Stainbrook
Caroline Bertrand: Interiors
Joyce Louie: Interiors

Recital hall

West façade

Lobby

East façade

Studio theater

Mary D. and F. Howard Walsh Center for Performing Arts

Texas Christian University
Fort Worth, Texas

Stone Type 1: limestone

Cut/Finish: sawn all sides

Size: 24" high x 5" thick x 4' long

Source: Garson, Manitoba, Canada

Quarrier/Fabricator: Gillis Quarries Ltd, Winnipeg, Manitoba, Canada

Stone Type 2: travertine

Cut/Finish: split-face front and ends, sawn top and bottom

Size: 12" high x 4" thick x 24" long

Design Team:
Malcolm Holzman: Partner-in-Charge
Nestor Bottino: Project Architect/ Manager
Kristopher Nikolich
Cleveland Adams
Steve Benesh
Eddie Kung
Michael Connolly
Geoff Thune
Catherine Minervini: Interiors

Associate Architect:
KVG/Gideon Toal, Inc.

Material Detail at Window
1   Cast in place concrete wall
2   Dovetail slot and anchor
3   Rigid insulation
4   Limestone
5   Clay tile
6   Aluminum window
7   Split-face travertine

Source/Quarrier/Fabricator: New Mexico Travertine, Belen, NM

Stone Type 3: granite

Cut/Finish: split-face front and ends, sawn top and bottom

Size: 8" high x 4" thick x random lengths

Source/Quarrier/Fabricator: Cold Springs Granite, Marble Falls, TX

Contractor: Thos. S. Byrne, Inc., Fort Worth, TX

Mason/Installer: CBC Masonry, Fort Worth, TX

Painting studio

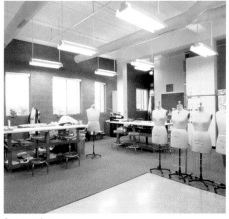
Costume shop

East façade

Art gallery

Studio theater

Del and Lou Ann Weber Fine Arts Building

University of Nebraska at Omaha
Nebraska, Omaha

Stone Type 1: limestone

Cut/Finish: split-face

Size: 8" high x 4" thick x random lengths

Source/Quarrier/Fabricator: Vetter Stone Company, Kasota, MN

Stone Type 2: granite

Cut/Finish: split-faced and polished

Size: 8" high x 4" thick x random lengths (split-face)
4" high x 4" thick x random lengths (polished)

Source/Quarrier/Fabricator: Dakota Granite Company, Milbank, SD

Contractor/Mason/Installer: Hawkins Construction

Design Team:
Malcolm Holzman: Partner-in-Charge
Robert Almodovar: Project Manager/ Project Architect
Ron Albinson
Nestor Bottino
Jonathan Cohn
Tony LaFazia
John Mariani
Todd Martin
Victor Rodriguez
Gilbert Sanchez
Bruce Spenadel
Matt Tendler
Dale Turner
Kristina Walker: Interiors

Associate Architect: The Schemmer Associates, Inc.

Lobby

Lobby

Entry walkway

Concert hall

Lyric theater

Lucille G. Lupe Murchison Center for Performing Arts

University of North Texas
Denton, Texas

Stone Type 1: limestone

Cut/Finish: split-face and sawn

Size: 8" high x 4" thick x random lengths

Source/Quarrier/Fabricator: TexaStone Quarries, Garden City, TX

Contractor: Huber Hunt & Nichols, Inc.

Mason/Installer: Wilkes Masonry

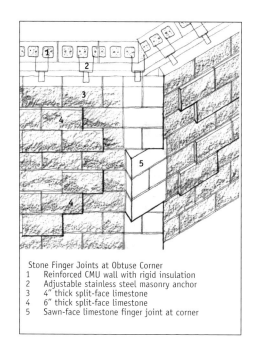

Stone Finger Joints at Obtuse Corner
1   Reinforced CMU wall with rigid insulation
2   Adjustable stainless steel masonry anchor
3   4" thick split-face limestone
4   6" thick split-face limestone
5   Sawn-face limestone finger joint at corner

Design Team:
Malcolm Holzman: Partner-in-Charge
Robert Almodovar: Project Manager/Architect
Carl Karas
Douglas Moss
Ky Mikagi
Jeff Neaves
Hakee Chang
Jeeyoon Lim
Caroline Bertrand: Interiors
Joyce Louie: Interiors

Associate Architect: Gideon Toal, Inc.

Stone monolith

Atrium from main stair

Atrium bridges

Entering student precinct

Third floor reading room

Information Services Building

Univesity of Otago
Dunedin, New Zealand

Stone Type 1: oamaru
Cut/Finish: split-face with saw cut border, split-face from quarry floor, cylindrical columns (smooth finish), and rough sawn (with circular disk pattern)

Size: 1350 mm x 700 mm x 200 mm (split-face with 100 mm saw cut border); 1400 mm x 710 mm x 450 mm (split-face from quarry floor) 800 mm diameter x 350 mm high (columns); 1200 mm x 703 mm x 300 mm (rough sawn)

Design Team:
Norman Pfeiffer: Partner-in-Charge
Stephen Johnson: Associate Partner
David Hart: Project Manager
Robin Kunz: Interiors

Associate Architect: Opus International Consultants

Source: Parkside Quarry, Oamaru, New Zealand

Quarrier/Fabricator/Mason/Installer: Dooleys Masonry, Oamaru, New Zealand

Stone Type 2: timaru bluestone

Cut/Finish: saw cut (smooth)

Size: 800 mm x 400 mm x 80 mm

Source: Timaru Quarry, Timaru, New Zealand

Quarrier/Fabricator: Timaru Bluestone Industries, Ltd., Timaru, New Zealand

Contractor: Naylor Love

Mason/Installer: Little and McCleod

Servery

Entry pavilion

Limestone finials

Refectory

Servery

McClurg Hall

Stone Type 1: sandstone

Cut/Finish: split and cut stone faces

Size: 8" high and 16" high x 8" thick x random lengths

Source/Quarrier/Fabricator: University of the South, Sewanee, TN

Stone Type 2: limestone

Cut/Finish: sawn

Size: 108" high x 30" thick x 30" long finials

University of the South Sewanee, Tennessee

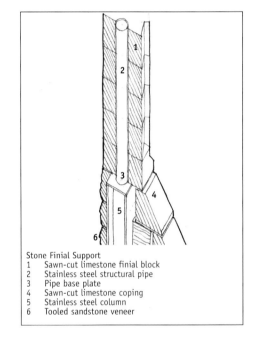

Stone Finial Support
1   Sawn-cut limestone finial block
2   Stainless steel structural pipe
3   Pipe base plate
4   Sawn-cut limestone coping
5   Stainless steel column
6   Tooled sandstone veneer

Source/Quarrier/Fabricator: Gillis Quarries Ltd, Winnipeg, Manitoba, Canada

Contractor: Orion Building Corporation

Mason/Installer: Brazos Masonry, Inc.

Design Team:
Malcolm Holzman: Partner-in-Charge
Robert Almodovar: Project Manager
Jeeyoon Lim
Mindy No
Robert Gross
Geoffrey Lynch
Ryan Bussard
Caroline Bertrand: Interiors

Lewis gallery

Marble hall

South façade

Lewis gallery

Marble hall

West Wing, Virginia Museum of Fine Arts

Richmond, Virginia

Stone Type 1: limestone

Cut/Finish: rusticated blocks, bull nose, sawn, and tooled

Size: 30" high x 8" or 12" thick x 48" long

Source/Quarrier/Fabricator: Indiana Limestone Company, Inc., Bedford, IN

Stone Type 2: granite

Cut/Finish: polished

Size: 30" high x 48" long

Contractor: Universal Construction Company, Inc.

Mason/Installer: Shenandoah Masonry

Design Team:
Malcolm Holzman: Partner-in-Charge
Pamela Loeffelman: Project Manager
Neil Dixon: Project Architect
Raoul Lowenberg: Construction Architect
Curtis Bales
Diane Blum
David Gross
Hilda Lowenberg
Robert Goesling
Darlene Fridstein: Interiors
Amy Wolk: Interiors

Stair detail

West façade

Newsroom

Production Studio

Interior circulation

WCCO -TV Communication Center and Headquarters

Minneapolis, Minnesota

Stone Type 1: limestone

Cut/Finish: top of ledge, honed, rockface, and tooled

Size: 30" high x 6" thick x 48" long, varied sills and lintels

Source/Quarrier/Fabricator: Vetter Stone Company, Kasota, MN

Contractor/Mason/Installer: McGough Construction Co., Inc.

Design Team:
Malcolm Holzman: Partner-in-Charge
John Lowery: Project Manager
Diane Blum
Violeta Dumlao
Jaime Fournier
Theron Grinage
Victoria Hammer
John Harris
Patricia Knobloch
Hilda Lowenberg
Mike McGlone
Lynne Redding
Candace Rosean

IMAX theater

Entrance

Lobby

Theater

Science Center

Whitaker Center for Science and the Arts

Harrisburg,
Pennsylvania

Stone Type 1: sandstone

Cut/Finish: split-face and chat sawn

Size: standard

Source/Quarrier/Fabricator: The Briar Hill Stone Co., Glenmont, OH

Contractor: Wohlsen Construction Company

Mason/Installer: Carretti, Inc.

Design Team:
Hugh Hardy: Partner-in-Charge
Stewart Jones: Project Manager
Jonathan Schloss: Project Architect
Jim Simmons: Construction Architect
Manuel Mergal
Yasin Abdullah
Juhee Lee
Alex Nussbaumer
Lou Kaufman
Chris Kaiser
John Mueller
Lucy Timbers
Caroline Bertrand: Interiors
Elizabeth Andrin: Interiors

Vetter Stone Company fabrication yard

BIOGRAPHY

Malcolm Holzman, FAIA
Founding Partner, HHPA

Malcolm Holzman's public buildings, described in a recent national publication as having a 'brash beauty,' are acknowledged for their evocative nature, technical vision and singular character. He has completed commissions in twenty-five states resulting in buildings that comprise some of this country's most notable architecture. His work shows a diversity of design solutions, which respond to varied programs, embrace a wide range of contexts, and incorporate regional materials.

In 2001, Mr. Holzman was the recipient of the first James Daniel Bybee Prize from the Building Stone Institute, which recognizes "a body of work distinguished by excellence in design," and the Gold Medal awarded by Tau Sigma Delta, the honor society for architecture and the allied arts. With his partners he has won more than a hundred awards including the Arnold W. Brunner Prize from the National Institute of Arts and Letters and the American Institute of Architects Firm of the Year Award.

In addition to enhancing the built environment through architecture, he regularly contributes to architectural publications. He has spearheaded the research efforts for the books Movie Palaces: Renaissance and Reuse and Reusing Railroad Stations. Mr. Holzman has orchestrated the publication of two HHPA monographs and a compendium of the firm's theater work. He currently serves as a member of the editorial board of The Mac Journal of the Mackintosh School of Architecture in Glasgow, as the American contributor to The Art Book, an international publication with reviews of newly published books about art, architecture and design.

Advocacy of architectural excellence has lead Mr. Holzman to hold endowed chairs at several schools of architecture including Yale University, the University of Wisconsin-Milwaukee, Ball State University and the University of Texas-Austin in addition to teaching specialized design studios at Lawrence Technical University and Rensselaer Polytechnic Institute.

As a leader in the profession, he has earned the designation of Fellow of the American Institute of Architects and election to the Interior Design Hall of Fame. Mr. Holzman has also served in many civic capacities including as trustee of both the Amon Carter Museum and Pratt Institute.

Mr. Holzman was born in Newark, New Jersey, in 1940 and received a Bachelor of Architecture Degree from Pratt Institute in 1963. He was later conferred its Distinguished Alumni Award for advancement of architecture and urbanism over a sustained period of time. Mr. Holzman founded Hardy Holzman Pfeiffer Associates in 1967 with Hugh Hardy and Norman Pfeiffer.

I have long felt the desire to record my passion for building with stone in words and pictures. Over the years, I casually discussed publication of a book about this expressive and accommodating material with family members, close friends and associates. Everyone was encouraging, but I felt the constraints of time were an insurmountable obstacle. The present opportunity occurred serendipitously: the subject arose in a conversation with Paul Latham, the publisher of a Hardy Holzman Pfeiffer Associates book, Theaters, whose immediate and enthusiastic response gave rise to this effort.

Several individuals at HHPA devoted considerable time in advancing this work. Debbi Waters' experience spearheading the firm's two prior books was extremely useful as she oversaw all aspects of this publication, from conception through production, in the most efficient and fun-loving way. Robert Almodovar, Nestor Bottino and Douglas Moss, associates directly involved with a number of the illustrated projects, offered valued commentary and provided sketches. Susan Packard's editing skills have seldom been tested to this extent; Heather Byron-Cox's dedication to reviewing drafts and checking factual details was admirable; and Jessica McCormack's and Gabrielle Bendiner-Viani's coordination of photography was nearly ceaseless.

ACKNOWLEDGMENTS

The enterprise would have been incomplete without the personal interest and professional skill of Henry Holtzman, who conceptualized the book's initial design, layout, and the graphics for its visual organization. Henry's generous contribution of talent and time was consequential to the book's evolution.

The stone suppliers Connie Edwards, Chuck Monson, Bruce O'Brien and Howard and Ron Vetter were kind enough to verify specific points about some of the projects. The Vetters also custom cut the stone from which the cover design is based. The designers Kevin Roche, Alex Madonna, and Garry Cunningham provided data about buildings of theirs cited in the text. Glenn Andres, Alex Bachrach, Ian Begg, Michael Kaplan,

Aimee Kriegsman, James Macaulay, Marvin Pate, Michael Reis and Wolfgang Toepfer—all friends and colleagues—were willing readers of various drafts and offered advice and encouragement. Tom Kessler revisited several of HHPA projects with his camera, while Gillis Quarries Ltd., Caithness Slate Products Ltd., and the Georgia Marble Company provided pictures of their operations.

Though it has been two years since we started out, this publication represents many hours of hard work. It pleases me to believe that it was a labor of love by individuals who shared my vision and understood my desire to promulgate stone's beauty and promise. I am profoundly grateful.

Peter Aaron: 30–31, 33, 182, 183

Robert Batey: 170

Craig Blackmon, AIA: 21, 22, 23, 24–25, 35, 38–39, 84, 85, 100–101, 102, 103, 104, 106, 107, 108, 110, 111, 160–161, 164–165, 166–167, 186, 192, 196

Erik Borg: 32, 180, 181, 182

Peter Brenner: 148, 157, 178, 179

Mike Brunton: 4–5

Ken Burris: 118–119

Michael Busselle/CORBIS: 8–13

Patricia Layman Bazelon: 59, 61, 62–63, 64, 198, 199

Cleveland Public Library Archives: 126

Whitney Cox: 198

Macduff Everton/CORBIS: 16, 26–27

Foaad Farah: 146

Kevin Fleming/CORBIS: 208–209

David Franzen: 20, 50, 51, 52–53, 163, 188, 189, 193

Michael Freeman/West Stock, Inc.: 14–15

George Heinrich: 94–95

HHPA: 43, 73, 98, 99, 104–105, 109, 130, 132, 138, 142–143, 145, 149, 150–151, 152, 172, 184, 187, 194, 195, 204–205

Malcolm Holzman: 17, 18, 19, 28, 29, 34, 42, 49, 60–61, 65, 72, 87, 89, 93, 97, 115, 116, 117

Timothy Hursley: 172

Jennie Jones: 124–125, 173

Henry Kalen: 70–71, 128–129, 140–141, 168–169

Tom Kessler: 6–7, 40–41, 44, 45, 46–47, 48, 68–69, 74, 75, 79, 112, 133, 134–135, 136–137, 174, 175, 176, 177, 190, 191

Christopher Lovi: 144

Norman McGrath: 88, 90-91, 92, 96, 121, 180, 200, 201

Courtesy of Georgia Marble Company: 122

Michael Moran: 80–81, 82, 83, 146, 147, 184, 185, 202, 203

Grant Mudford: 153, 156, 178

Enzo & Paolo Ragazzini/CORBIS: 66

Cervin Robinson: 36–37, 54, 55, 56–57, 58, 76–77, 78, 123, 127, 142, 158–159, 170, 171, 172, 198

Steve Rosenthal: 131

The Images Publishing Group: 120

Denny Tillman: Cover, Title pages, 206

Tim Street-Porter: 154–155

Tiziana and Gianni Baldizzone/ CORBIS: 86

Endpapers (from left to right):
First Row: Craig Blackmon, AIA; Malcolm Holzman; Tom Kessler; Tom Kessler; David Franzen; Patricia Layman Bazelon
Second Row: Peter Aaron; Cervin Robinson; Patricia Layman Bazelon; Norman McGrath; Craig Blackmon, AIA; Tom Kessler
Third Row: Tom Kessler; Craig Blackmon, AIA; David Franzen; David Franzen; Cervin Robinson; Tom Kessler

PHOTOGRAPHY CREDITS